Green **Line** 3
Das Trainingsbuch

von
Pauline Ashworth

Klett Lerntraining

Zu diesem Trainingsbuch gehört eine Audio-CD. Mit ihrer Hilfe lernst du, Englisch besser zu verstehen. Die Texte sind im Buch mit dem Symbol 🎧 gekennzeichnet. Wenn du die Diktate und Lückendiktate schreibst, benutze die Pausentaste, um Zeit zum Schreiben zu haben. Viel Erfolg!

Sprecher: Breakspeare, Jane; Ellmann, Vanessa; Ellmann, Alison; Khalil, Louai; Martin, Benjamin; Turner, Adrian; Vollmer, Amelie; Vollmer, Dominik; Vollmer, Marie Louise; Walker, Amy; Walker, Zack
Produktion: Ton in Ton Medienhaus, Stuttgart

Bibliografische Information der Deutschen Nationalbibliothek
Die Deutsche Nationalbibliothek verzeichnet diese Publikation in der Deutschen Nationalbibliografie; detaillierte bibliografische Daten sind im Internet über http://dnb.dnb.de abrufbar.

Das Werk und seine Teile sind urheberrechtlich geschützt. Jede Nutzung in anderen als den gesetzlich zugelassenen Fällen bedarf der vorherigen schriftlichen Einwilligung des Verlages. Hinweis zu §52a UrhG: Weder das Werk noch seine Teile dürfen ohne eine solche Einwilligung eingescannt und in ein Netzwerk eingestellt werden. Dies gilt auch für Intranets von Schulen und sonstigen Bildungseinrichtungen. Fotomechanische Wiedergabe nur mit Genehmigung des Verlages.

10. Auflage 2018

© PONS GmbH, Stöckachstraße 11, 70190 Stuttgart 2009. Alle Rechte vorbehalten.
www.klett-lerntraining.de

Redaktion: form & inhalt verlagsservice Martin H. Bredol / Linda Strehl
Zeichnungen: Naomi Fearn, Berlin; Katja Rau, Fellbach: S. 36, 41, 80; Barbara Gerth-Mohr, Hamburg: S. 56 oben; Elsie Lennox, London: S. 56; David Norman, Meerbusch: S. 125
Umschlaggestaltung: Koma Amok, Stuttgart
Umschlagfoto: Ariel Skelly/Corbis; Mauritius Images GmbH
Satz: klartext, Heidelberg
Reproduktion: Meyle+Müller GmbH+Co. KG, Pforzheim
Druck: Gebr. Geiselberger GmbH, Altötting

Printed in Germany
ISBN 978-3-12-929976-0

Inhalt

Unit 1

Sportarten	6
Die Bedeutung neuer Wörter erschließen: Verben und Substantive	8
Mit dem zweisprachigen Wörterbuch arbeiten	9
Wichtige Ausdrücke: Zustimmen und ablehnen	9
Wiederholung: Verlaufsform und einfache Form der Gegenwart	10
Wiederholung: Futurformen	11
Das *simple present* zur Wiedergabe der Zukunft	12
Das *present progressive* zur Wiedergabe der Zukunft	13
Zuhören: Gegenwart oder Zukunft?	14
Das *will future* zum Ausdruck von spontanen Entscheidungen	15
Zuhören: Gegenwart oder Zukunft?	15
Notwendige Relativsätze	17
Contact clauses	18
Relativsätze mit *whose*	19
Zuhören: *who's* oder *whose?*	19
Präpositionen im notwendigen Relativsatz	20
Sports	22
Informationen heraussuchen	23
Detailverständnis	24
Schreiben	24
Zuhören und das Wesentliche verstehen	25
Zuhören: Wörter, die man beim Sprechen verbindet	25
Zuhören: Fußball für Mädchen?	26

Unit 2

Bauwerke und Gebäude	27
Das viktorianische England	27
Aus Englands Geschichte	28
Stoffe und Erzeugnisse	28
Verben aus dem Wortfeld „Sprechen"	29
Adjektive: Antonyme	29
Verben mit französischen Wurzeln	30
Wichtige Wendungen: Vorschläge machen	30
Wiederholung: Die modalen Hilfsverben	31
Die modalen Hilfsverben und ihre Ersatzverben	32
Das Plusquamperfekt	35
Lesen: Mit unbekannten Texten umgehen	37
Zuhören: Satzmelodie	41
Zuhören: Ein Besuch im Tower of London	41
Zuhören: Ein Ausflug nach London	42

Revision A (Unit 1–2)

Kreuzworträtsel verkehrt herum	43
Verben + Objekt	44
Adjektive	44
Die Zukunft	45
Das Plusquamperfekt	45
Relativpronomen	46
Modale Hilfsverben und ihre Ersatzverben	46
Kommunikationsübung	47
Hörverstehen: Wer hat gewonnen?	48
Schreiben: Tennisstars	48

Unit 3

Menschen beschreiben	49
Kollokationen	49
Theater	50
Zwei-Wort-Verben	51
Wichtige Wendungen	52
Die Pronomen auf -self/-selves (Reflexivpronomen)	53
Zuhören: Die Pronomen auf -self/-selves	55
Each other	56
Wiederholung: Bedingungssätze – Typ 1	57
Bedingungssätze – Typ 2	58
Bedingungssätze – Typ 3	60
Ein Theaterstück	62
Zuhören: Wordstress	65
Zuhören und das Wesentliche verstehen	65
Hörverstehen: Telefongespräche	66
Zuhören: Drei Telefongespräche	66

Unit 4

Der Nordwesten Englands	67
Nationalitäten	67
Verben	68
Wortgitter	69
Adjektive	69
by/until	70
Wichtige Wendungen: Jemandem helfen/sich entschuldigen	70
Wiederholung: Adjektiv oder Adverb?	71
Wiederholung: Possessivpronomen	72
Der bestimmte Artikel	73
Der unbestimmte Artikel	74
Das Adjektiv als Substantiv	75
Adjektive nach bestimmten Verben	76
Das Futur II	78
Paarwörter	80
Reading skills: Sachtexte	81
Zuhören: Aussprache	86

Zuhören und richtig reagieren	86
Zuhören: Ein Umzug	87

Revision B (Unit 3–4)

Go, get, make oder take?	88
Zwei-Wort-Verben	88
Odd one out	89
Relativpronomen	89
Bedingungssätze	90
Die Zukunft	90
Übersetzung	91
Finde die Fehler	91
Zuhören und Notizen machen	92
Sprechen: Jemandem helfen/sich entschuldigen	92
Zuhören, lesen und schreiben	93

Unit 5

Medien	95
Beim Casting	96
Verben	97
Ein Unfall	97
Menschen	98
Adjektive	98
Wiederholung: Das Perfekt und die einfache Form der Vergangenheit	99
Das Passiv	100
Vom Aktiv ins Passiv	102
Weitere Zeitformen des Passivs	103
Das Passiv bei Verben mit zwei Objekten	105
Lesen und schreiben: Zeitungsberichte	107
Zuhören: Strong and weak sounds	110
Zuhören: Media in your life	110
Zuhören: Vorschläge machen	111

Unit 6

Auf Reisen	112
Menschen	113

To take	113	Zuhören: gleicher Klang, andere	
Verben	114	Schreibung	129
Adjektive: Situationen beschreiben	114	Zuhören: Ein Notfall	129
Verben für *to say*	115	Zuhören: Smalltalk	130
Verben und Substantive in der gleichen Form	115	**Revision C (Unit 5–6)**	
Direkte und indirekte Rede	116		
Indirekte Rede mit Zeitverschiebung	117	Menschen	131
Zuhören und Wiedergeben	118	*Odd one out*	131
Zeitangaben in der indirekten Rede	119	Kollokationen	132
Zuhören und das Wichtigste berichten	120	*Mixed bag*	132
		Das Passiv	133
Die indirekte Rede mit Einführungssatz im Präsens	121	Indirekte Rede	134
		Zuhören und sich Notizen machen	135
Fragen in der indirekten Rede	122	Mediation: Ein Unfall in England	136
Indirekte Aufforderungssätze	124		
Zuhören und berichten	125		
Lesen: Ein Segelurlaub	126	**Lösungen**	138

Unit 1

Sportarten

1 Sieh dir die Bilder an und beschrifte sie. Welche Sportarten zeigen sie?

1.

a) o _____ b _____

b) r _____

c) p _____

→ r _____

2.

a) t _____ r _____

b) u _____

c) c _____

→ t _____

3.

a) g _____

b) i _____

c) s _____

→ i _____

4.

a) b _____

b) h _____

→ c _____

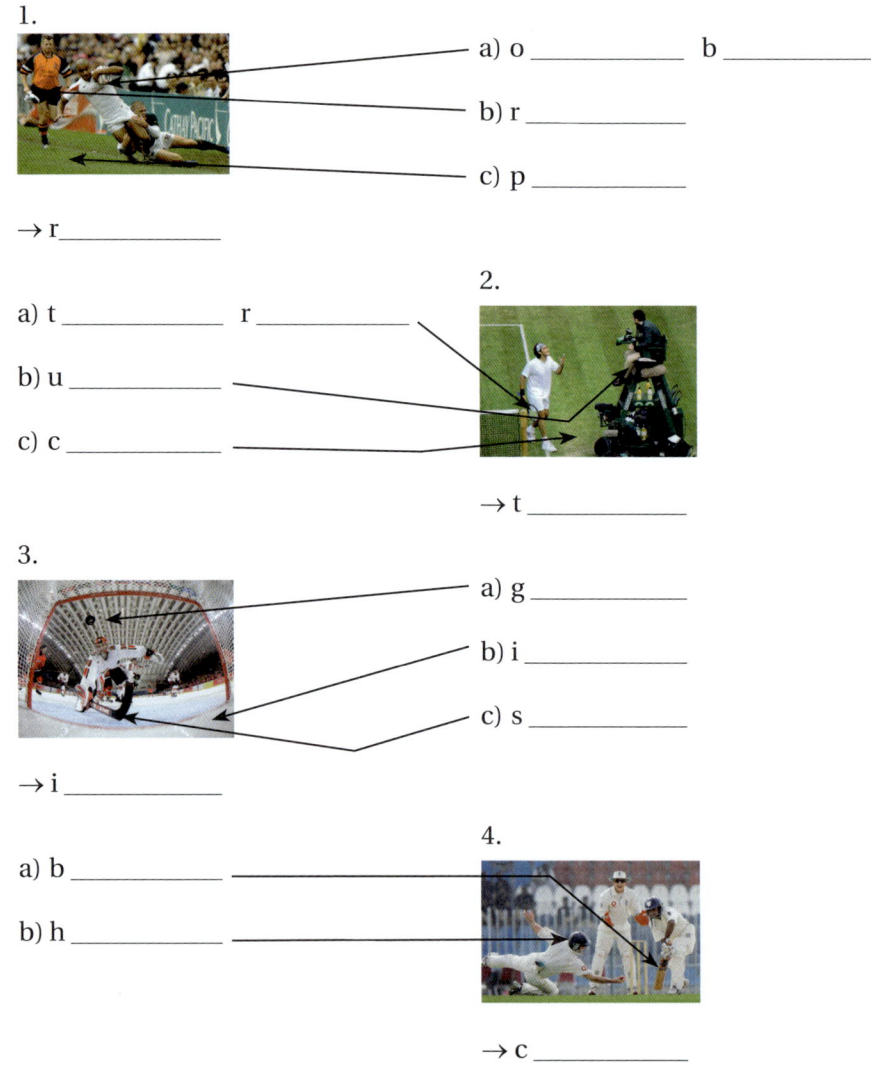

Wortschatz 1

2 Lies den Text und löse die Worträtsel (Anagramme) auf, dann setze die richtigen Wörter in den Text ein.

sbae – babasell – ourct – felid – heltem – chpit – craes – crakte – suler – sickt – atrck

It is not always easy to talk about sport in the English-speaking world – there are so many different words for the same thing. When you play tennis, you hit the ball with a _____, when you play _____, you hit the ball with a bat and when you play hockey, you hit the ball with a _____. When you play baseball, you run from one _____ to another on a _____, but you play rugby on a _____ and tennis on a _____. And if you are an athlete, you run _____ on a _____.

We use the same words to mean different things, too. If you play football in the USA, you wear a _____. Irish football has yet different _____.

3 Lies die Definitionen durch: Welche Sportart wird jeweils beschrieben? Aus den hinterlegten Buchstaben kannst du zum Schluss eine weitere Sportart zusammensetzen.

1. American kids who wanted to surf in towns started this sport. _ _ _ _ _ _ _ _ _ _ _ _
2. When you do a lot of sport, you get this on your body. _ _ _ _ _
3. This is a very old race in which you have to run a very long way. _ _ _ _ _ _ _ _
4. People who win races at the Olympics win one of these. _ _ _ _ _ _ _ _
5. If you run faster than anybody else has ever run, then you will win this. _ _ _ _ _ _
6. You can use these to get down mountains in the winter. _ _ _ _

A sport: _____

Die Bedeutung neuer Wörter erschließen: Verben und Substantive

4 Skifahren! Werden die farbig gedruckten Wörter als Nomen oder Verb verwendet?

1. The world is getting warmer and there is less snow every winter. _____

2. But in some places you can even ski in the summer. _____

3. It isn't easy to jump with skis on. _____

4. It's great fun and dangerous to have a race down a mountain. _____

5 Schreibe diese Sätze neu, indem du das Verb in ein Substantiv umwandelst.

1. She jumped really high.   *Her jump* _____

2. He kicks the ball very hard.   _____

3. Will it snow enough this year? _____

4. The rowing boat crashed.   _____

6 Manchmal kann ein Wort Verb und Substantiv zugleich sein bzw. mehrere Bedeutungen haben. Wähle aus, welche Übersetzung die richtige ist.

1. You shouldn't **race** everywhere. You'll have an accident.

   a) (sich) hetzen ☐   b) Rennen ☐   c) rennen ☐

2. I always liked the **slides** in playgrounds when I was a child; now I like the bobsleigh.

   a) Dia ☐   b) Rutsche ☐   c) rutschen ☐

3. You don't need big **waves** to go surfing.

   a) winken ☐   b) wehen ☐   c) Wellen ☐

Mit dem zweisprachigen Wörterbuch arbeiten

7 Suche aus deinem Wörterbuch die jeweils richtige Übersetzung für die Verwendung von *channel* heraus.

1. He's going to swim the channel tomorrow. → _____

2. What channel is the football on? → _____

3. We need to channel our energy into our work. → _____

8 Welches englische Wort würdest du für die farbigen Wörter verwenden?

1. Ich muss deinen Skipass kontrollieren. → _____

2. Wenn ich zu schnell fahre, kann ich die Skier nicht kontrollieren. → _____

3. Du sollst ihn nicht schlagen. → _____

Wenn du nicht sicher bist, ob du die richtige Übersetzung im Wörterbuch gewählt hast, mache die Probe, indem du diese wiederum im anderen Teil des Wörterbuchs nachschlägst!

Wichtige Ausdrücke: Zustimmen und ablehnen

9 Bilde aus den angegebenen Wörtern sechs verschiedene Sätze, die deine Zustimmung bzw. Ablehnung ausdrücken, und ordne sie der richtigen Spalte zu.

I – agree – don't – be – think – that's – true – what – too – silly

agreeing	disagreeing
_____	_____
_____	_____
_____	_____

Wiederholung: Verlaufsform und einfache Form der Gegenwart

Das **simple present** verwendest du,
- wenn etwas immer wieder passiert oder immer wahr ist:
She doesn't **play** rugby.
- wenn du ein Geschehen wiedergibst:
They **get up** early and **go** skiing while the snow is good.

Signalwörter: *always, often, never, sometimes*

Das **present progressive** verwendest du,
- wenn gerade etwas passiert:
Look! We**'re winning** the match.
What **are** you **doing** now?
We **aren't meeting** today.

Signalwörter: *Look! now, at the moment, today*

10 John ruft Gemma an, die gerade bei einem Kricketspiel zusieht. Ergänze die richtige Zeitform des Verbs.

John: Hi Gemma. How _____ (it/go)?

Gemma: Oh, fine. We _____ (just/have) a picnic.

John: No, I mean in the game. _____ (they/play) well?

Gemma: Oh, the game! I don't know. I _____ (not/understand) it at all. The man _____ (hit) the ball and then sometimes he _____ (run) and gets points but sometimes he _____ (not/run) at all and he gets more points.

John: Gemma. _____ (you/not/know) the rules?

Gemma: Of course not. Girls _____ (not/play) cricket at school.

John: So why did you go?

Gemma: Well, my brother bought the tickets and the picnic and I _____ (love) picnics.

Grammatik 1

Wiederholung: Futurformen

Das **going to future** und das **will future** verwendet man beide, um auszudrücken, dass etwas in der Zukunft passieren wird. Aber:

Das **going to future** verwendest du, wenn du

– einen Plan oder eine Absicht äußerst:	He**'s going to go** rowing next week. We**'re going to learn** some new tricks on the skateboard.
– du etwas vorhersehen kannst durch Anzeichen, die es jetzt schon gibt:	It's very cloudy and cold. It**'s going to snow** later. We**'re going to lose** the game.

Das **will future** verwendest du, wenn du

– etwas vorhersagen willst, worauf du keinen Einfluss hast:	The weather **won't be** good today. People **will** always **play** football.
– deine Meinung abgibst. Dabei benützt du z. B. *I'm sure*, *I promise* oder *I think*.	I think we**'ll win** the competition. I hope it **won't snow** later.

11 Beim Tennis. Trage die richtige Form der Zukunft in die Lücken ein.

Wendy: Look! Yvonne is tired now. Liz _____ (win) the match.

Chris: I don't know. Look at those clouds. We _____ (have) a storm soon and then they _____ (stop) the match.

Wendy: I hope they _____ (not/stop) stop the match. Liz only needs to win two more games.

Chris: Did you phone Tim? _____ (you/meet) him later?

Wendy: Yes, I called him. He _____ (come) here at three and we _____ (play) tennis. Do you want to play, too?

Chris: Oh, I think I _____ (go) home. I don't want to get wet.

11

Das *simple present* zur Wiedergabe der Zukunft

Du verwendest das **simple present**, wenn du über feste Termine in der Zukunft redest, z. B. über Zeitangaben in Fahrplänen oder Programmen. Man nennt das *simple present* daher auch **timetable future**.

The match **starts** at 8 o'clock.
His train **leaves** at half past three.
What time **does** it **arrive**?

12 Lies die Sätze durch. Beziehen sie sich auf das *present* oder das *future*?

1. The competition starts at two o'clock. _____
2. Harry's train arrives at eleven on Monday. _____
3. The trains always arrive late. _____
4. When do you arrive at the tennis club on Fridays? _____

13 Ein Skiurlaub. Unterstreiche die richtige Form der Zukunft.

Jake: You're going on your skiing holiday on Saturday, aren't you? How do you / are you going to get there?

Susan: We fly / 're going to fly. The plane leaves / will leave really early in the morning and so I hope we aren't going to / won't miss it.

Jake: And what time do you / will you arrive home again?

Susan: At 8 pm on the next Saturday. I hope I'll be / 'm good at skiing by then.

Jake: Well, I hope you won't / aren't going to break your leg on the first day.

Susan: No, I won't. The plane will arrive / arrives at 10 o'clock but then we have to get on a coach so we won't / aren't going to arrive until about 4 o'clock.

Das *present progressive* zur Wiedergabe der Zukunft

Du verwendest das *present progressive*, wenn du über **Vereinbarungen** redest, vor allem wenn schon **Zeit und Ort ausgemacht** sind:

What **are** you **doing** at the weekend? – I**'m meeting** John in town on Saturday. We**'re going** to the cinema.

Das *present progressive* zur Wiedergabe der Zukunft ist dem *going to future* sehr ähnlich. In vielen Fällen können beide verwendet werden. Wenn du jedoch sagen willst, dass eine **Entscheidung** getroffen wurde, die **Details** aber noch **nicht** ausgemacht sind, verwendest du eher das *going to future:*

Are **you going to phone** Bill? (Hast du dich schon dazu entschieden?)
I'**m going to learn** to ski. (Ich weiss aber noch nicht, wann und wo.)

14 Ein sportliches Wochenende. Schau dir die Bilder und Wörter an und formuliere Sätze im *present progressive*.

weekend

What – you? _____

_____

I – Saturday

Pete – Sunday

_____

we – watch

_____

1 | Wortschatz | Grammatik | Leseverstehen | Hörverstehen

Zuhören: Gegenwart oder Zukunft? 🎧 1

15 Höre dir zunächst die Kurzdialoge auf der CD an. Dann entscheide dich: Beziehen sich die gesprochenen Sätze auf das *present* oder das *future*?

1. a) What are you doing? _____

   b) I'm meeting Tina. _____

2. He's playing tennis with some mates. _____

3. a) Where are you going? _____

   b) I'm going to my athletics club. _____

   c) No, some friends are coming to my house at 8 pm. _____

16 Am Wochenende. Lies den Text und vervollständige die Lücken mit der richtigen Form von *simple present* oder *present progressive*.

Tim: _____ (you/go) to Brighton for the marathon tomorrow?

Mike: Yes, _____ (short answer). I _____ (go) by bus.

Do you want to come with me? The bus _____ (leave)

at twelve.

Tim: What time _____ (the bus/arrive)?

Mike: It _____ (arrive) about 12.30.

Tim: That's very early. The marathon _____ (not/start)

until three o'clock.

Mike: Yes, but I _____ (meet) Pete at one so we can get warm first.

Tim: Why do you want to get warm first?

Mike: Didn't you know? We _____ (run) in the marathon.

Grammatik 1

Das *will future* zum Ausdruck von spontanen Entscheidungen

Du verwendest das **will future**, wenn du spontan deine **Hilfe** anbietest oder um Hilfe bittest oder wenn du spontan etwas **entscheidest**.

The telephone's ringing. – Oh, I**'ll get** it.
These bags are heavy. – Oh, I**'ll carry** them for you.
There's somebody at the door. **Will** you **see** who it is, please?

17 Ein Skiurlaub. Bilde Kurzdialoge, indem du die Sätze verbindest.

I can't ski.	Will you show me?
I'm so cold.	I'll teach you.
I know the way.	I'll get you a bigger size.
These ski boots are too small.	Will you lend me some?
You don't have enough money.	I'll lend you my jacket.

Zuhören: Gegenwart oder Zukunft? 2

18 Höre dir die Kurzdialoge auf der CD an und vervollständige die Sätze. Bei welchen handelt es sich um spontane Entscheidungen?

spontane Entscheidung

1. Oh, I _____ with you. ☐
2. Oh, I'm sure you _____ win. ☐
3. No, I _____ football with my friends then. ☐
4. _____ it to me? ☐
5. I _____ you some new ones. ☐
6. I _____ in the 100 metres. ☐
7. I _____ 13 next Friday. ☐

19 Skateboarden. Überlege, was du auf die Aussagen hin antworten könntest. Benutze die richtige Zeitform: *will future* oder *simple present*?

1. I'd love to go skateboarding but I haven't got a skateboard.

(I/lend/my skateboard) _____

2. Those tricks are great. How often do you practise?

(practise/every evening) _____

3. I'm practising for a competition next weekend.

(sure/you/win) _____

20 Beim Kricketspielen. Vervollständige die Lücken mit den richtigen Zeitformen der angegebenen Verben.

Tim: We _____ (play) cricket at six but we need more players.

Mike: Oh, I _____ (play) with you. I like cricket.

Tim: OK. Well, we _____ (meet) at six in the park so I _____ (see) you there. And _____ (you/go) to the cricket match tomorrow, too?

Mike: I don't know. What time _____ (start)?

Tim: It _____ (start) at ten and _____ (finish) about five.

Mike: Well, I can't go until one. I _____ (have) a skiing lesson.

Tim: A skiing lesson? But I'm sure it _____ (not/snow) before then.

Mike: No, I know but I _____ (go) to the new ski centre and it's inside.

Notwendige Relativsätze

Mit einem notwendigen Relativsatz wird ein Wort **näher beschrieben**. Ohne ihn wäre der Sinn des Hauptsatzes unklar.

Personen:	*subject*	
I like the teacher	**who/that**	teaches us sport.
I don't know anybody	**who/that**	can ski well.
Dinge:	*subject*	
Rugby is a game	**which/that**	is very popular in Britain.
He won a competition	**which/that**	is held every two years.

Who bezieht sich nur auf Menschen, **which** nur auf Dinge, **that** kann sich auf Menschen oder Dinge beziehen.

Vor einem notwendigen Relativsatz steht *kein* Komma, und beim Sprechen gibt es *keine* Pause zwischen Hauptsatz und Relativsatz.

21 Worauf musst du beim Skifahren achten? Ergänze *who* oder *which*.

1. You need to wear clothes _____ will stay warm and dry.

2. You should use skis _____ aren't too long.

3. It's good if you can find a teacher _____ can explain well.

4. Try to find a place _____ usually has lots of snow in the winter.

5. Some places are good for people _____ are just learning.

22 Im Skiurlaub. Formuliere vollständige Sätze mit *who* oder *which*.

1. borrowed some skis – skis were too small

   I_____

2. paid for a lesson with a teacher – he was terrible

   _____

3. went skiing down a hill – very scary

   _____

Contact clauses

Wenn das Relativpronomen **Objekt** („wem?", „wen oder was?") des Relativsatzes ist, kann man es **weglassen**. Solche Relativsätze heißen *contact clauses*.

	object	subject		
The sport The sport	which/that	I I	like best is golf. like best is golf.	… **den** ich …
Is he the boy Is he the boy	who/that	you you	beat you at tennis? beat at tennis?	… **den** du …

23 Golfspielen. Markiere beim ersten Lesen die Relativpronomen. Dann lies den Text nochmals und streiche die Relativpronomen durch, die man nicht unbedingt braucht (also wenn sie Objekt des Relativsatzes sind).

Golf is a sport which is very popular in England but it is not a sport that most people think is very exciting. In fact there are people who think that golf isn't a sport at all because they think of old people who walk slowly around a big field or two and every ten minutes or so hit a ball. I was once one of those people. I'm a person who loves most sport but I thought that golf was very boring. How wrong I was! A friend who I've known for years and loves golf bought me a lesson for my birthday. It was a present which I didn't really want but you can't say no, can you? And I'm glad I didn't say, "No, thank you," because it was one of the best presents that I've ever had. I loved the lesson and I've loved golf ever since. It's great fun when you play with people who you like and it keeps you fit. You often walk ten kilometres or more around golf courses which are very hilly while you are carrying a bag which is very heavy.

24 Tennis. Trage das richtige Relativpronomen ein – aber nur, wenn man es unbedingt braucht.

1. Tennis is a sport _____ kings once played. There were even queens _____ played tennis.

2. Wimbledon is a tennis competition _____ is famous all over the world. There is sometimes a problem there with rain _____ stops the games.

3. Boris Becker was a tennis star _____ people still know now.

Relativsätze mit *whose*

> Relativsätze können auch durch **whose** + Nomen eingeleitet werden.
>
> I know a boy **whose** brother plays for United. … einen Jungen, **dessen** Bruder …
>
> Some children **whose** parents want them to be famous start very young. … Kinder, **deren** Eltern …
>
> Football clubs **whose** stars are very famous make lots of money even when they lose. … Vereine, **deren** Stars …
>
> Mit *whose* drückst du einen **Besitz** aus. Man kann es für Menschen oder Dinge verwenden.
>
> Achtung: Verwechsle *whose* nicht mit *who's* (= who is)!

25 Erfolgreich im Sport? Unterstreiche das richtige Relativpronomen.

People which/who/whose become very good at sport have to train very hard for many years. It helps if they have a sports club which/who/whose is good in their area. And it's always easier for children which/who/whose friends like sport, too. There are also people which/who/whose have bodies which/who/whose are better for one sport or another. For example, people which/who/whose legs are longer are often better at running. And, of course, for some sports it's easier for children which/who/whose parents can buy them good equipment or lessons.

Zuhören: *who's* oder *whose*? 3

26 Höre zu. Hörst du *who's* oder *whose*?

1. _____   2. _____

3. _____   4. _____

Präpositionen im notwendigen Relativsatz

Im notwendigen Relativsatz steht die Präposition (*with*, *to*, *for*) meistens hinter dem Verb.

That's the boy **who/that** I practise **with**. | … der Junge, **mit dem** …

That's the racket **which/that** I'm interested **in**. | … der Schläger, **für den** …

Wenn das Relativpronomen weggelassen wird *(contact clause)*, steht die Präposition immer hinter dem Verb.
That's the boy I practise **with**.
That's the racket I'm interested **in**.

Im förmlichen Stil kannst du die Präposition auch vor das Relativpronomen stellen, aber nur bei *which* oder *whom*.
That's the boy **with whom** I practise.
That's the racket **in which** I'm interested.

27 Ein bekannter Tennisspieler. Bilde aus zwei Sätzen einen Hauptsatz mit Relativsatz.

1. I wrote to a tennis player. He went to my school.

   <u>The tennis player</u>

2. I've kept the letter. He answered my questions in it.

3. He sent me an old racket. He played with it once.

4. He's the tennis star. We are now all waiting for him.

5. We're having a lesson from the nicest tennis star – I have ever heard of him.

Leseverstehen 1

28 *The London Olympics.* Schreibe diese *contact clauses* um, indem du die Präposition vorziehst.

1. That's the swimming pool the Olympic swimmers will swim in.

   _____

2. He's an athlete we'll hear a lot about.

   _____

3. That's the road they will run the marathon on.

   _____

4. Here are some runners everybody will want to talk to.

   _____

29 Memoiren eines Tennisspielers. Schau dir die Bilder und Wörter dazu an und formuliere Relativsätze mit oder ohne Präposition.

1. won first game with it

2. practised with

3. first – gave interview to

4. his father taught me to play

1. *That's the* _____

2. *That's* _____

3. _____

4. _____

21

Sports

30 Lies die Texte durch. Welcher Sport wird jeweils beschrieben?

1. This is a very old game which is played mostly in English-speaking countries. When you go to English villages in the summer, you often see some people, usually men, who are playing the game on the village green, which is an area of grass in the middle of the village. There are eleven players on each team and the men usually wear white. They play the game with bats and a ball and it is quite a slow game. It is a game which is difficult to understand and it often looks like nothing is happening.

→ _____

2. This is a very popular game in the USA; maybe the most popular game in the country. Two teams which have nine players each play the game with bats and a ball. They often wear helmets because the ball is very hard. A player hits the ball and then has to run from one base to another. When they run all the way round and touch all four bases, they score a run. The game started about 200 years ago in North America and it is a little like an English game which is called rounders. People sometimes call the game hardball because of the hard ball and there is another game which is almost the same; softball. Women play softball and the ball is not as hard as the ball which the men use.

→ _____

3. This is another very old game which people have played all over the world. There are pictures which are over 4000 years old which show people who are playing this game. People think that the modern game started in Canada in about 1870. Two teams which each have six players on the ice at one time play with long sticks and try to score goals. The game is most popular in countries which are cold in winter and in which the water in lakes becomes ice for a few months every year.

→ _____

Wenn du einen Text lesen sollst, ist es nicht nötig, gleich jedes einzelne Wort zu verstehen oder nachzuschlagen. Übe stattdessen, einen Text, egal wie schwer er dir vorkommt, erst einmal durchzulesen und die Wörter, die du nicht kennst, zu ignorieren. Beschäftige dich mit den Einzelheiten erst beim zweiten Lesen!

Informationen heraussuchen

31 Die Fragen beziehen sich auf die Texte in Übung 30. Versuche sie zu beantworten, ohne den Text noch einmal zu lesen.

Text 1:

1. How many players are there on each team? _____

2. What colour do they usually wear? _____

3. In which countries do they play this sport? _____

Text 2:

4. How many players are there on each team? _____

5. What other name does this sport have? _____

Text 3:

6. How old are the oldest pictures which show this sport? _____

7. What is the weather often like in countries which play this? _____

Detailverständnis

32 Korrigiere die falschen Sätze.

Text 1: This game is very fast but it isn't hard to understand.
_____

Text 2: Players score runs when they run from one base to another.
_____

Text 3: Only people who live in countries which are cold play this game.
_____

Schreiben

33 Verfasse mithilfe der Notizen eine Kurzbeschreibung der Sportart Fußball.

- two teams
- eleven players on each team
- players kick ball and score goals
- very old game
- played all over the world
- modern football started in England

_____
_____
_____
_____
_____

Zuhören und das Wesentliche verstehen 🎧 4

34 Höre dir die Radioreportagen an, dann beantworte die Fragen dazu.

1. What sport is he watching in 1? _____

2. What does Henry break? _____

3. What sport is he watching in 2? _____

4. What does Williams have a problem with? _____

5. What sport are they watching in 3? _____

6. What does the player run past? _____

35 Vervollständige die Sätze aus der ersten Reportage.

Yes, he's _____ to _____ it. Is it going to _____ a new world record?

_____ broken the _____ record in the 400 metres.

Zuhören: Wörter, die man beim Sprechen verbindet 🎧 5

36 Lies dir die Sätze durch und überlege, welche Wörter du beim Sprechen zum nächsten hinüberbinden würdest, dann höre dir den Text auf der CD an und bezeichne die Stellen mit einem Bogen wie im Beispiel angegeben.

I'm not‿an athlete but I love unusual sports.

I love skateboarding in the park and surfing on the sea.

I'm not very good at sport but I enjoy it.

I've had lots of accidents of course, but I've never broken anything.

Zuhören: Fußball für Mädchen? 6

37 Höre dir die Diskussion über Fußball an, dann beantworte die Fragen.

1. Welche dieser Zusammenfassungen passt am besten zu der Diskussion?
a) Ann and Sally are trying to decide which sport is best; hockey or football. They decide that football is the best sport.
b) Ann wants to play football at school and thinks it isn't fair that girls can't play. Sally agrees with her and they decide to start a football team.
c) Ann likes football much better than hockey and thinks it isn't fair that girls can't play football at their school. Sally disagrees.

→ _____ passt am besten.

2. Verbinde die Sätze so, wie sie im gesprochenen Text vorkommen.

But, Ann, no other girls want to play football.	Oh, don't be silly.
Football's a sport which is hard and dangerous.	Yes, you're right.
That's the only way the other players can stop you.	Rubbish.
… football's just so much more fun than hockey.	That's not true.
They haven't got the skill.	Yes, I agree with you.

3. Sind diese Aussagen *true* oder *false*? Korrigiere die falschen Aussagen.

a) Ann thinks that football is more dangerous than hockey. _____

b) Ann thinks that many girls aren't very good with a hockey stick. _____

c) Sally likes to watch football. _____

d) Both girls think that women are better than men at football. _____

e) Ann has the idea to start a football team. _____

Korrektur: _____
_____

Unit 2

Bauwerke und Gebäude

1 Sieh dir die Bilder an und beschrifte sie.

1. _____ 2. _____ 3. _____ 4. _____

Das viktorianische England

2 Lies den Text und ergänze die Wörter richtig.

Queen Victoria's r _ _ _ _ began in 1837 and ended in 1901 when she died. This time is now called the Victorian A _ _ and it was an important time in British history.

When Victoria came to the t _ _ _ _ _, the British E _ _ _ _ _ was still very big although the American c _ _ _ _ _ _ _ had already become i _ _ _ _ _ _ _ _ _ _. The colonies made Britain very rich because they gave Britain cheap raw m _ _ _ _ _ _ _ _ and food. The I _ _ _ _ _ _ _ _ _ Revolution had already begun and this also helped to make Britain richer still. The Industrial Revolution started because lots of new i _ _ _ _ _ _ _ _ _ like the steam e _ _ _ _ _ meant that people could make things very fast in factories. It made Britain rich but its factories also made lots of people poorer. People who had worked at home now had to work in the factories and live in s _ _ _ _.

Aus Englands Geschichte

3 Löse das Kreuzworträtsel und setze aus den hinterlegten Buchstaben das Lösungswort zusammen.

1. Queen Victoria was the … of India.
2. A … was not a Catholic.
3. A … worked for rich people in their houses.
4. A … fought for his king usually on a horse.
5. King Harold was a …
6. A … works on the land and sometimes has animals.
7. A … killed King Harold and became king.
8. A … is a rich man and his wife is usually a lady.

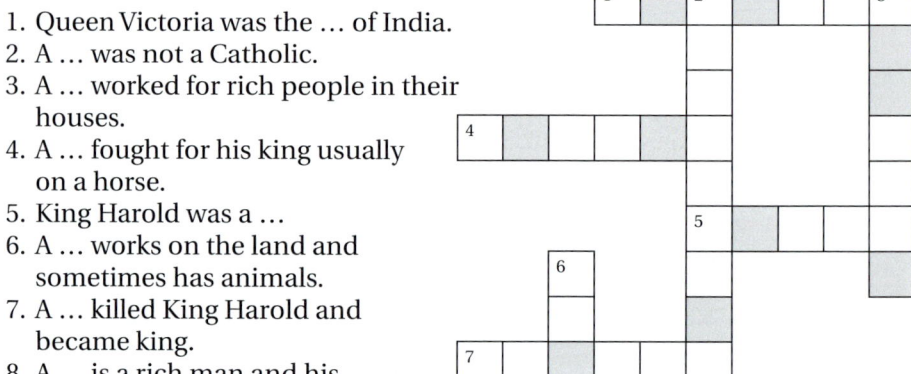

→ Queen Victoria became the g _ _ _ _ - g _ _ _ _ _ _ _ _ _ _ of many kings and queens.

 **Tipp** Erstelle für deine/-n Freund/-in ein Kreuzworträtsel. Kann er/sie es lösen?

Stoffe und Erzeugnisse

4 Aus welchen Rohstoffen werden welche Dinge gemacht? Verbinde.

wax   steam engines

gold   candles

steel   tables

wood   jewellery

Verben aus dem Wortfeld „Sprechen"

5 Lies erst den Text durch, dann trage die Verben, die am besten passen, in die Lücken ein.

| to continue | to gasp | to joke | to reply | to wonder |

"What is William of Normandy doing now?" _____ King

Harold. "Do you think we can beat him now?" he asked.

"No, we need more rest," _____ a knight. King Harold

looked angry and looked at the other knights. They looked at the floor.

"The men have just walked all the way from the north. They need a

rest," _____ the first knight.

King Harold didn't want to hear any more and he took out a knife.

"You've … you've killed me," _____ the knight.

"Well, now you can have a nice long rest," _____ King Harold.

Adjektive: Antonyme

6 Bilde aus dem Buchstabensalat Wörter, die das Gegenteil der genannten Wörter bedeuten.

aclen – feer – dmoner – moraln – relpy – socle

old-fashioned _____   strange _____

dirty _____   question _____

expensive _____   far _____

Verben mit französischen Wurzeln

7 Die folgenden französischen Wörter gibt es so ähnlich auch im Englischen. Wie lauten sie?

attaquer → _____

continuer → _____

répliquer → _____

suggerer → _____

préparer → _____

Wenn du neue Wörter siehst oder lernst, überlege, ob sie dir bekannt vorkommen: Vielleicht kennst du sie schon aus dem Deutschen, dem Französischen oder Lateinischen?

Wichtige Wendungen: Vorschläge machen

8 Ein Ausflug. Bilde mithilfe der Wörter Sätze in der richtigen Wortreihenfolge, um Vorschläge zu formulieren.

about – London – a – how – trip – to – ?

_____

Theatre – could – see – go – we – and – Globe – the

_____

go – suggest – I – we – by – Tube

_____

timetable – get – shall – I – the – ?

_____

30

Grammatik 2

Wiederholung: Die modalen Hilfsverben

Can, may, must und ihre Verneinungen, *can't, may not, mustn't* und *needn't*, sind modale Hilfsverben. Du kannst sie nur im *simple present* verwenden, mit der Ausnahme von *could*, das eine Vergangenheitsform ist.
Nach *can, may* und *must* steht immer die Grundform des Verbs ohne *to*. Die Form der *modals* ist für alle Personen gleich.
May ist sehr förmlich und wird meist in Fragen verwendet.

He **can** speak French. She **could** read when she was two.	Er kann Französisch sprechen. Sie konnte lesen, als …
He **can't** read yet.	Er kann noch nicht lesen.
Can/May I have an ice-cream?	Darf ich ein Eis haben?
You **can't/mustn't** swim in that river.	Du darfst nicht in …
I **must** call Jill before she goes out.	Ich muss Jill anrufen, bevor …
I **needn't** go to bed yet.	Ich muss noch nicht ins …

9 Ein Besuch im Globe Theatre. Übersetze die Sätze.

1. Ich kann die Schauspieler dort gut verstehen.

   _____ the actors there very well.

2. Wir müssen nicht die ganzen Zeit auf unseren Plätzen sitzen.

   _____ in our seats all the time.

3. Du musst eine Eintrittskarte kaufen.

   _____

4. Wir dürfen keine Fotos machen.

   _____

5. Ihr dürft herumlaufen.

   _____

Die modalen Hilfsverben und ihre Ersatzverben

> Weil man die modalen Hilfsverben nur im *present tense* verwenden kann, benutzt man in den anderen Zeitformen die Ersatzverben **be able to, be allowed to** and **have to**.
>
> can (not) → to (not) be able to ([nicht] können):
> Most people in England **are able to/can speak** English. *(present)*
> Most people in England **couldn't/weren't able to speak** English in the eleventh century. *(past)*
>
> can/may → to be allowed to (dürfen)
> **May/Can/Am** I **allowed to take** a photo? *(present)*
> **Will** we **be allowed to talk** to the actors later? *(future)*
>
> can't/may not/mustn't → to not be allowed to (nicht dürfen)
> You **mustn't/can't/may not talk** loudly in a library. *(present)*
> We **weren't allowed to go** to bed late last night. *(past)*
>
> must → to have to (müssen)
> We **must/have to learn** French. *(present)*
> We **have had to learn** French for three years. *(present perfect)*
>
> needn't – don't have to (nicht müssen)
> I **needn't/don't have to get up** before eight. *(present)*
> I **won't have to go** to bed early next weekend. *(future)*

10 Ergänze zu den modalen Hilfsverben das passende Ersatzverb und umgekehrt. Achtung: Manchmal gibt es mehrere Möglichkeiten!

must	_____	can *(dürfen)*	_____
can *(können)*	_____	have to	_____
needn't	_____	mustn't	_____
be able to	_____	be allowed to	_____
not have to	_____	may	_____

11 Ein Besuch in London. Welcher Satz aus der Auswahl ist bedeutungsgleich? Nenne den Buchstaben.

1. We mustn't drive on the right. → _____
a) We aren't able to drive on the right.
b) We aren't allowed to drive on the right.
c) We don't have to drive on the right.

2. May I go to the cinema? → _____
a) Am I allowed to go to the cinema?
b) Do I have to go to the cinema?
c) Am I able to go to the cinema?

3. We needn't walk everywhere. → _____
a) We aren't able to walk everywhere.
b) We aren't allowed to walk everywhere.
c) We don't have to walk everywhere.

12 Königin Elisabeth I. Gib ihre Gedanken wieder: Was konnten, durften, sollten … sie oder andere tun oder nicht tun?

1. I can speak five languages.
2. Drake may attack the Spanish.
3. Drake must not keep all the gold.
4. I needn't go to the theatre.
5. The theatre must come to me.

1. Elizabeth _____ five languages.

2. Drake _____ the Spanish.

3. Drake _____ all the gold.

4. Elizabeth _____ to the theatre.

5. The theatre _____ to her.

13 Urlaub in England. John und Sarah aus den USA erzählen. Setze die passenden Ersatzverben ein.

We've had a great holiday and lots of things have been different. Usually when we buy things in the shops, we needn't think too hard but here we _____ try hard to understand people. Usually we can understand everything on TV but we _____ in England. Usually we must go to bed early but on holiday we _____ go to bed before 11 pm. And usually we can't get up late – our mother doesn't let us stay in bed after 7 am – but on holiday we _____ stay in bed until lunchtime. But, of course, on holiday we've wanted to get up early.

14 Mary träumt von der Zeit, wenn sie endlich erwachsen sein wird. Übersetze.

Ich werde nach Hause kommen können, wann ich möchte.
_____ when I want to.

Ich werde das Essen kochen dürfen, das ich auch essen möchte.
_____ the food which I want to eat.

Aber vielleicht werde ich es nicht kochen können?
But maybe _____ it?

Ich werde keine Hausaufgabe machen müssen, aber ich werde arbeiten müssen.
_____

Ich werde nicht mehr in die Schule gehen dürfen. Schade!
_____. What a pity!

34

Das Plusquamperfekt

> Wenn du sagen möchtest, dass etwas vor etwas anderem in der Vergangenheit passiert ist, verwendest du das *simple past perfect*.
>
> When I arrived at the museum, it **had** already **closed**. ≈ The museum closed first and then I arrived there.
>
> She was late for school because she **had missed** the bus. ≈ She missed the bus and then she was late at the museum.
>
> Das *past perfect* wird mit *had* und dem *past participle* gebildet und ist für alle Personen gleich. Es wird oft zusammen mit dem *simple past* verwendet.

15 Im Theater. Formuliere die Sätze um, indem du das *past perfect* verwendest.

1. I heard the Globe Theatre was interesting and so I visited it.

→ I _____ the Globe Theatre because I _____

that it was interesting.

2. We visited the theatre and then we bought some tickets.

→ We _____ some tickets for a play after we _____

_____ the theatre.

3. I didn't read a book by Shakespeare and then we saw the play.

→ When we _____ the play, I _____

a book by Shakespeare.

4. The play started and then we arrived.

→ The play _____ when we _____ at the theatre.

5. I saw the play and then I wanted to become an actress.

→ After I _____ the play, I _____ to become an

actress.

2 | Wortschatz | Grammatik | Leseverstehen | Hörverstehen

16 Was passiert auf den Bildern? Formuliere Sätze mit dem *past perfect*.

1. The bus _____ when she _____ the bus stop.

leave – got to

The play _____ _____ before she _____ at the theatre.

2. start – arrive

3. The Tower of London _____ _____ when she _____ about it.

close – think

17 Die Römer. Vervollständige die Lücken mit der richtigen Form des *simple past* oder *past perfect*.

The Romans _____ (defeat) a lot of Europe and North Africa when they _____ (attack) England for the second time. They _____ (build) Hadrian's Wall after they _____ (fight) the Scots for years. When the Romans _____ (leave) England, they _____ (build) many roads and fine buildings. As soon as the Romans _____ (leave), other people _____ (attack) England. Later everybody forgot what they _____ (learn) from the Romans.

Lesen: Mit unbekannten Texten umgehen

Vorbereitung:
Schon bevor du anfängst, den Text zu lesen, solltest du versuchen, möglichst viel im Vorfeld herauszufinden. Sieh dir z. B. die Überschrift oder die Bilder im Text an: Worum geht es überhaupt?

Das erste Mal lesen – das Wesentliche verstehen:
Lies zunächst den Text einfach durch, um grob zu verstehen, wovon er handelt. Halte dich nicht damit auf, unbekannte Wörter nachzuschlagen, damit du nicht vom Wesentlichen abgelenkt wirst.

Das zweite Mal lesen – Detailverständnis:
Lies den Text noch einmal, um mehr über den Inhalt herauszufinden. Jetzt kannst du wichtige Wörter nachschlagen – trotzdem ist es nicht nötig, jedes einzelne Wort zu verstehen.

18 Schau dir die Überschrift und die Bilder auf den folgenden Seiten an. Wovon könnte die Geschichte handeln? Dann lies die Geschichte ein erstes Mal und wähle die beste Zusammenfassung.

Time to change
I'd just milked the cows when Elizabeth arrived. She wasn't smiling. She hadn't smiled a lot in the last few weeks. I'd asked her if something was wrong but she hadn't told me. Today she looked unhappier than ever and
5 didn't speak at all. Then we heard a loud noise and I ran outside. Elizabeth ran to me. She was scared. Every time a train went past, she ran to me and I held her close. I loved the trains and she hated them. "They're so loud and noisy and dirty," she shouted. "Why did somebody invent them? Why does everything have to get worse all the time?"
10 "What's wrong?" I asked.
"Oh Sam! It's terrible. We don't have enough work … or money or food. We have to go to Manchester and work in a factory," she shouted and she cried and cried.
"No, you can't go," I shouted loudly, "You can stay with me. I can look after
15 you."
"Oh, you know you can't. You're only 14 and you only have enough food for your family. And anyway I have to help look after my little
20 brothers and sisters."
She went home and I didn't see her for the next few days. When I went to look for her, her house was

empty. There was nobody and nothing there. They had taken everything; tables, chairs, beds. Everything was gone. I sat on the floor and cried. She hadn't even said goodbye.

I had to find her again but Manchester was so far away and I couldn't take our horse. I couldn't get there and she was right; I couldn't look after her. I tried to forget her but how can you forget your best friend? I worked hard on the farm but that became more difficult, too. We had enough food for us but we couldn't sell much because most of the people in the area had moved away … to Manchester.

One day, a few months later, my father decided to take some of our young cows to a market in Manchester and sell them and he let me go with them.

It took hours to walk there and when we got there, I was very tired, but I didn't sit down; I went to find Elizabeth. I had been to Manchester last year but everything was different now. There were even more factories there and so many streets full of slums. I walked and walked but I didn't find Elizabeth. I sat down for a few minutes and then I heard a train. I was near a station. A real station! I'd never seen a station before. I was really excited and I ran there. A train had just arrived and I went to look at the 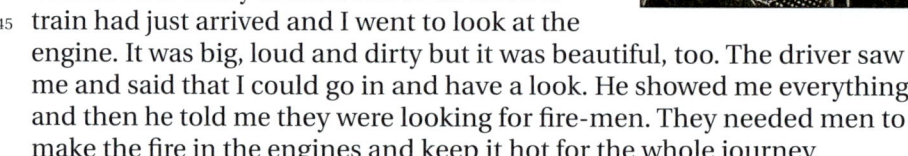 engine. It was big, loud and dirty but it was beautiful, too. The driver saw me and said that I could go in and have a look. He showed me everything and then he told me they were looking for fire-men. They needed men to make the fire in the engines and keep it hot for the whole journey.

"I can do that. I'm sure I can do it," I shouted.

"Well, come back and talk to the boss tomorrow," he said.

Now I just had to ask my father. He wasn't happy.

"Sam, I'm not going to give my son to those black monsters," he shouted. "It's not normal. It can't be healthy to move so fast."

"But Dad! They pay well and maybe I can learn to be a driver and then I'll get more money. Trains are the future, Dad. You have to let me go."

He let me go. I moved to Manchester and I lived in a very small house with a driver and his family. It was a hard job but I loved it. Every Sunday when I didn't have to work, I looked for Elizabeth. At first I just walked through the streets but then I had a good idea: I just had to try all the churches. So every Sunday I tried a different church in Manchester. I was really lucky and just two months later, I was sitting in church when I saw Elizabeth's father. He looked terrible. What had the factories done to him? And where was Elizabeth? I looked around to find her but she wasn't there. I was scared that something had happened to her.

"She's not here. She's working in a factory outside Manchester. She had to go and it's better there than here," her father told me afterwards.

Her father told me where to find the factory and the Sunday after that I walked there. It took me three hours but I found her. She was working in
70 the garden when I saw her and I stood and watched. She looked well, better than her father. She'd had enough to eat. When she saw me, she looked up and smiled and then ran to me. When she'd finished work, we sat and talked for two hours. She gave me some food from the garden and she told me that she could read and write now. She'd learned it at the school there.
75 Every day she had to work in the factory and then in the garden. In the evening she had lessons at school. Some of the other girls fell asleep but she loved it and never slept in a lesson.
After that we met every Sunday. I walked three hours there, spent some time with her and then walked three hours back home again. She taught
80 me to read and write and that's how I got a job as a train driver. We got married two years later.

mögliche Zusammenfassungen:
a) Sam lives on a farm in the country. Elizabeth is happy when her family moves to the town because there are many exciting jobs there. Sam doesn't want her to go.
b) Sam and Elizabeth live in the country. Elizabeth's family doesn't have enough work and they all have to go and work in a factory. Sam goes to Manchester and gets a job on the trains. He finds Elizabeth again.
c) Sam loves trains and wants to be a driver. Elizabeth hates them so she leaves Sam and goes to the city. She gets a job in a factory and learns to read and write.

→ Zusammenfassung _____ ist richtig.

19 Nun lies die Geschichte nochmals. Sind diese Aussagen *true, false* oder *not in the text*? Korrigiere die falschen Sätze.

	true	false	not in the text
1. Elizabeth was unhappy because they had to move to Manchester.	☐	☐	☐
2. Elizabeth didn't like trains because they were new.	☐	☐	☐
3. Elizabeth and her family walked to Manchester.	☐	☐	☐
4. Sam moved to Manchester because he had a job there.	☐	☐	☐
5. Sam found Elizabeth in a church.	☐	☐	☐
6. Elizabeth didn't want Sam to work on the trains.	☐	☐	☐

Korrektur: _____
_____
_____

20 Mehrdeutige Wörter. Wähle die Bedeutung aus, die die Wörter im Text haben.

1. past (l. 6)   a) nach ☐   b) Vergangenheit ☐   c) vorbei ☐

2. move (l. 57) a) bewegen ☐   b) sich bewegen ☐   c) umziehen ☐

3. take (l. 69) a) nehmen ☐   b) dauern ☐   c) bringen ☐

4. look up (l. 71) a) aufsehen ☐   b) nachschlagen ☐   c) hinaufschauen ☐

21 Welche Sätze im Text haben die gleiche Bedeutung wie die Sätze unten? Suche sie heraus.

1. "You aren't able to look after me."

_____

2. I knew that everything had changed because I went to Manchester last year.

_____

3. The train driver saw me and I was allowed to go in and look at the train.

_____

4. She gave me something to eat and then said, "I can read and write now."

_____

Zuhören: Satzmelodie 🎧 7

22 Lies dir die Sätze durch. Welche Wörter würdest du besonders betonen? Dann höre dir den CD-Track an und unterstreiche die Wörter, die betont werden.

The Romans weren't able to keep the Scots out of England so they built Hadrian's Wall.

King Harold's army had had to walk for miles before they fought the battle against William of Normandy.

Queen Elizabeth the First was a very popular queen for a long time but at the end the people became unhappy with her.

Tipp: Wenn du wichtige Wörter in einem Satz betonst, versteht dein Gesprächspartner besser, was du meinst. Versuche, die Sätze oben mit verschiedenen Betonungen auszusprechen!

Zuhören: Ein Besuch im Tower of London 🎧 8

23 Höre dir den Dialog auf der CD an, dann stelle die Sätze in die richtige Reihenfolge, indem du sie nummerierst.

_____ Calvin went to the toilet.

_____ He saw a ghost.

_____ He sat down and had a drink and a sandwich.

_____ Calvin's class went down to the dungeons.

_____ Calvin looked in some dungeons and found a door.

_____ The dungeon door closed.

_____ The ghost showed him the way out.

_____ His teacher found him.

2 | Wortschatz | Grammatik | Leseverstehen | Hörverstehen

Zuhören: Ein Ausflug nach London 9

24 Mary und ihre Freunde sprechen über ihre Pläne fürs Wochenende. Du hörst zuerst ihre Diskussion *(part 1)*, dann Mary an einer Kasse *(part 2)*. Ordne die Sätze unten richtig zu: Werden sie in *part 1* oder *2* gesprochen? Dann höre dir den CD-Track noch einmal an und prüfe, ob du recht hattest.

Excuse me. _____

Well, how about a trip to London? _____

And where can I get a brochure, please? _____

Are we allowed to take photos in the theatre? _____

How much are the tickets, please? _____

And why don't we check what's on at the theatre, too? _____

We could go to the Science Museum. _____

Yes, that's a good idea. _____

… how should we get there? _____

We'd like to see Romeo and Juliet this afternoon, please. _____

Shall I get a timetable? _____

Are there special prices for children? _____

25 Noch einmal CD-Track 9: Welche Aussage ist richtig? Unterstreiche.

They want to go to London by bus/tram/train.

They want to buy some tickets for the train/theatre on the Internet.

They buy three/five tickets which cost five/33 pounds at the theatre.

They needn't/mustn't take photos in the theatre.

Revision A (Unit 1–2)

Kreuzworträtsel verkehrt herum

1 Schau dir das bereits ausgefüllte Kreuzworträtsel an. Dann erstelle aus den Satzteilen die passenden Fragen zu den Lösungsworten, indem du sie mit Linien verbindest.

			¹j	e	w	²e	l	³l	e	⁴r	y
						m		u		a	
						p		n		c	
	⁵t		⁶a			r		g		k	
	h		t			e		s		e	
	r		h			s				t	
⁷g	o	g	g	l	e	s					
	n		e								
	e		t				⁸l				
		⁹s	e	r	v	a	n	t			
							d				
		¹⁰c	o	l	o	n	y				

1. This is something
2. This is a woman
3. These are things
4. This is something
5. This is something
6. This is a person
7. These are things
8. This is a woman
9. This is a person
10. This is a country

who can run, throw or jump.
who lives in a rich person's house and works for them.
who has an empire.
which swimmers or ski jumpers wear.
which everybody needs and swimmers need big ones.
which has to give its raw materials to another country.
who is married to a lord.
which a queen or king sits on.
which you need when you want to play tennis.
which you can wear.

Revision A — Rückblick / Ausblick

Verben + Objekt

2 Ordne die Verben einem passenden Objekt zu.

attack, clean, continue, control, feed, flap, nod, open

_____ a new building   _____ a horse

_____ your speed   _____ a house

_____ your arms   _____ your head

_____ an enemy   _____ a journey

Adjektive

3 Löse die Anagramme auf und ergänze die Adjektive richtig.

socle, acext, reef, dermon, lova, sualunu

I've just seen a game of American football. Somebody gave me a _____ ticket, so I went to the match. It's an _____ game in England and I'd never seen a match before, so I was excited. They played it with an _____ ball, like rugby. But it's more _____ than rugby – people have played rugby for a long time. I'm surprised how many people were interested in the game – I'm sure, there were over 1000 there, although I don't know the _____ number. And they all wanted to have a _____ look at this strange game. It wasn't bad but I don't believe it'll ever become popular.

Die Zukunft

4 Ein Tagebucheintrag. Unterstreiche die richtigen Formen der Verben.

I meet/'m meeting Albert again tomorrow. I love him and we've already planned everything. First we're going to/'ll travel on a train. I'm so excited. I've never been on a train before. I hope I'm not going to/won't be scared. Then we're watching/'ll watch a horse race. The horse race starts/is starting at three o'clock and I hope that I don't/won't miss the first race. One of my horses is going to/will start in it and he's probably going to/'ll probably win – he's a great horse. I'd like to ride a horse, too, but I can't, of course. Women can't do things like that. When I'm Queen, I change/'ll change all that. Yes, my uncle is ill and he's dying/'s going to die soon. Then I'll be/'m being Queen. Queen Victoria. Sounds good, doesn't it?

Das Plusquamperfekt

5 Ein Skateboard-Turnier. Formuliere mithilfe der Notizen ganze Sätze.

1. I learnt some tricks – then I saw the poster

    → When I _____ the poster, I _____ some new tricks.

2. the competition started – I arrived

    → The competition _____ when I _____.

3. I practised for two minutes – I broke my board

    → I _____ for two minutes when I _____ my board.

4. I borrowed a skateboard – I won the competition

    → After _____ a skateboard, I _____ the competition.

Revision A

Relativpronomen

6 Gib die Sätze mit *who, which* oder *whose* wieder. Dann lies deine Lösung nochmals durch und klammere die Relativpronomen ein, wenn man sie auch weglassen könnte.

1. Queen Elizabeth was a queen. Most English people liked her.

   _____

2. She was a queen. Her pirates stole treasure from the Spanish.

   _____

3. Mexico was a country. It had lots of gold and silver.

   _____

4. Mexico was a country. Spain brought the treasure from there.

   _____

5. England was a country. Spain attacked it.

   _____

Modale Hilfsverben und ihre Ersatzverben

7 Queen Victoria erzählt von sich. Vervollständige die Lücken.

I didn't enjoy being Queen. I _____ (must not) do what I

wanted and I _____ (must) be nice to people. I _____

_____ (may) learn lots of things but I _____

(can/never) ride a horse. I _____ (needn't) worry

about money but I _____ (must not) spend it all.

No, that wasn't a great job.

Kommunikationsübung

8 Du bist mit deiner Mutter in London. Ihr möchtet ins Science Museum gehen. Da deine Mutter nicht besonders gut Englisch spricht, musst du zwischen ihr und dem Mann an der Kasse vermitteln. Übersetze jeweils!

Mutter: Frag ihn bitte, was die Eintrittskarten kosten.

Du: _____

Mann: Oh, it's free.

Du: _____

Mutter: Das ist ja schön. Können wir auch ins 3D-Kino *(3D cinema)* gehen?

Du: _____

Mann: Yes, but you have to buy a ticket for that.

Du: _____

Mutter: OK. Frag ihn, wo wir eine Broschüre über das Museum kaufen können.

Du: _____

Mann: I've got one here. Here you are.

Mutter: Oh. Thank you. Ähm, dürfen wir hier Fotos machen?

Du: _____

Mann: You're allowed to take photos in some rooms. You can see signs there.

Du: _____

Mutter: Gut. Kannst du ihn fragen, wie wir zum Café kommen?

Du: _____

Mann: Yes, it's over there, but you can also have picnics here in the museum.

Du: _____

Revision A Rückblick Ausblick

Hörverstehen: Wer hat gewonnen? 🔊 10

9 Höre dir den Dialog auf der CD an, dann stelle die Sätze mit Ziffern in die richtige Reihenfolge.

_____ Mike's team scored a goal in the right goal.

_____ The other team scored a goal in the right goal.

_____ The other team scored a goal in the wrong goal.

_____ The referee's watch stopped.

_____ They had an argument about who won.

Schreiben: Tennisstars

10 Verbessere den Text: Mache aus zwei Hauptsätzen Hauptsatz + Relativsatz und verwende das Plusquamperfekt, wenn möglich.

Venus and Serena Williams are sisters. They are famous tennis champions. Their father was the man – he taught them to play tennis. Before they went to the tennis court, their father watched a video. He found lots of tips on the video.
The Williams' family grew up in an area of Los Angeles. It was a poor area. Their father wanted them to do well at sport so that they could have a better life. They worked hard. They won lots of matches before they were even 14 years old.

48

Unit 3

Menschen beschreiben

1 Wie könnte man die folgenden Menschen beschreiben? Suche aus der Wortschlange die richtigen Adjektive heraus.

1. Mark always keeps the best for himself. He's _____.

2. Robert doesn't like anybody to look at his girlfriend. He's _____.

3. I don't like Sheila. She often gets angry when I talk to her and I don't know why. She's _____.

4. Jane is no fun. She's never happy. She's always _____.

5. Chris is only 15 but he often gives good advice. He's very _____.

Kollokationen

2 Ergänze die passenden Verben.

I cannot _____ a lie. James _____ me crazy. I don't know if I love him or hate him. When I know that I will see him, I _____ dressed very carefully. I think I like him and I think he likes me, too. I'll have to _____ sure or I will _____ crazy. OK. I've _____ a decision. I'm going to ask him out … Or maybe not! Help!

3 | Wortschatz | Grammatik | Leseverstehen | Hörverstehen

Theater

3 Beschrifte das Bild.

a) _____
b) _____
c) _____
d) _____
e) _____
f) _____

4 Ein Theaterstück. Setze die Wörter in der passenden Form ein.

| applauded | cast | costumes | director | put on | rehearsals | rehearse |

We _____ a play last week at school. It was great fun but very hard work. We wrote the play ourselves and it was only short but we still had to _____ a lot. First we all had to learn our parts and then we had about ten _____ with all the _____. My friends were the actors and actresses and I was the _____ because I can't act at all. We didn't need _____ because the play was about life at school. It was a funny play – or we thought so anyway. We weren't quite sure if everybody else thought it was funny until the audience _____ at the end. Then we knew that everybody else enjoyed it, too.

Wortschatz 3

Zwei-Wort-Verben

5 Beziehungsprobleme. Ergänze die richtige Präposition.

I'm going to split _____ with Lucy tomorrow. We don't get _____ any more. She doesn't listen _____ me and she never turns _____ the TV. I will turn _____ a couch potato if I stay with her. Tomorrow I'm going to put _____ my best clothes, eat _____ my dinner and then tell her. I feel sorry _____ her, of course, but you know; that's life. And anyway I'm going to go out _____ her best friend when I've called her.

6 Suche die passenden Übersetzungen aus dem Wortgitter heraus und ordne sie ihrer Übersetzung zu.

w	t	u	l	a	w	w	i	s	h
e	r	d	e	c	i	d	e	o	u
m	a	n	a	g	e	d	s	k	n
a	n	t	v	h	z	x	r	m	e
r	s	f	e	l	r	a	n	a	a
r	l	q	s	t	a	n	d	w	r
y	a	b	v	l	d	r	b	h	n
j	t	c	o	n	t	a	c	t	i
b	e	h	a	v	e	f	q	u	j
k	e	u	a	y	s	c	h	a	t

schaffen _____

hinterlassen _____

übersetzen _____

heiraten _____

sich benehmen _____

entscheiden _____

verdienen _____

erreichen _____   wünschen _____

ertragen _____   plaudern _____

Wichtige Wendungen

7 Diplomatisch diskutieren: Vervollständige die Sätze.

Y _ _ ' _ _ g _ _ a p _ _ _ _ , b _ _ …

T _ _ _ ' s t _ _ _ , b _ _ …

I d _ _ ' _ m _ _ _ t _ _ _ , b _ _ …

I k _ _ _ , b _ _ …

I g _ _ _ _ y _ _ ' _ _ r _ _ _ _ , b _ _ …

Sprich die Sätze mehrfach laut aus: Irgendwann rollen sie wie von selbst von der Zunge.

8 Am Telefon. Verbinde die Satzteile zu vollständigen Sätzen.

1. I'm just calling to say   me back, please?

2. Could you call   it for me, please?

3. Can I take   I'll be home late.

4. Can you spell   speak to Chris.

5. Hope to hear   from you soon.

6. I'd like to   a message?

9 Welchen der Sätze aus Übung 8 kann man benutzen, wenn man auf einen Anrufbeantworter spricht?

Es eignen sich die Sätze _____ .

52

Die Pronomen auf -self/-selves (Reflexivpronomen)

Du kannst die Pronomen auf -self/-selves als Reflexivpronomen oder als verstärkende Pronomen verwenden.

reflexiv:

I can look after **myself**.	... auf mich *selbst* aufpassen.
Don't hurt **yourself**.	Tu *dir* nicht weh.
He/She/The cat washes **himself/herself/itself**.	Er/Sie/Die Katze wäscht sich.
Let's make **ourselves** some lunch.	Machen wir *uns* etwas zum Mittagessen.
Help **yourselves** to some food.	Nehmt *euch* vom Essen.
They only think of **themselves**.	Sie denken nur an *sich*.

Die Reflexivpronomen sind Objekt im Satz und beziehen sich immer auf das Subjekt. Viele Verben, die im Deutschen reflexiv sind, sind im Englischen nicht reflexiv, z. B.: He's **changed**. – Er hat *sich* verändert. **Sit down!** – Setzen Sie *sich!*

verstärkend:
Mit den Pronomen auf -self/-selves kannst du auch betonen, dass jemand etwas **selbst** getan hat.
I made that cake **myself!**
Did you really paint your room **yourselves?**

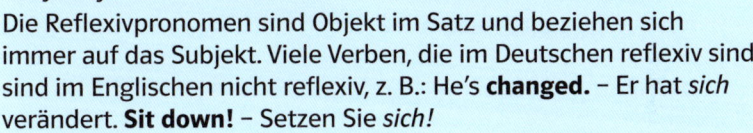

10 Trage die richtigen Reflexivpronomen ein.

I've just hurt _____.

Bye everybody! I hope you all enjoyed _____.

She often talks to _____.

They made that CD _____.

Jane! Remember to behave _____ at your grandma's.

Achtung bei *you:* Verwendest du es für eine *(yourself)* oder mehrere *(yourselves)* Personen?

11 Ein ganz normaler Tag? Streiche die Reflexivpronomen durch, wo man sie nicht benötigt.

It was Friday. I got up and then got dressed myself as always. I was late and had to hurry myself, as always. I went to school, worked hard and behaved myself – as always! I got home, sat down myself and relaxed myself – as always. My dad made dinner and hurt himself with a knife – as always. I ate dinner and got ready myself for youth club – as always – on a Friday! When I got to youth club, I met myself a girl. We laughed and enjoyed ourselves. I felt myself happy – as always. But nothing now was as always – everything had changed itself.

12 Schreibe die farbig markierten Sätze mit dem Pronomen auf *-self/-selves* neu, um das Subjekt zu verstärken.

Hey, you two. This card is really nice. Did you really make it?

_____

That poem's great and guess what! John wrote it.

_____

Will you ask him for me? I don't want to ask him.

_____

Ann! I'm not helping you. You have to find it.

_____

We're hungry. Can we cook dinner?

_____

Zuhören: Die Pronomen auf -self/-selves 11

13 Höre dir die Sätze auf der CD an. Welche Pronomen hörst du? Trage sie ein. Dann überlege: Werden sie verstärkend oder reflexiv verwendet? Kreuze an.

Pronomen	verstärkend	reflexiv
1. _____	☐	☐
2. _____	☐	☐
3. _____	☐	☐
4. _____	☐	☐
5. _____	☐	☐
6. _____	☐	☐

14 Ein Theaterstück. Übersetze die Sätze.

Wir haben das Stück selbst geschrieben.

_____

Alle haben sich fertig gemacht.

_____

Wir mussten uns beeilen.

_____

Ich war die Regisseurin und konnte mich nicht entspannen.

_____

Aber alle hatten Spaß.

_____

Each other

Wenn du sagen willst, dass zwischen Personen etwas wechselseitig passiert, verwendest du *each other*.

They often help **each other**.	Sie helfen **einander**.
They met **each other** at 8.30.	Sie trafen **sich** um 8.30.
They looked at **each other**.	Sie schauten sich **gegenseitig** an.

Verwechsle nicht *each other* und *themselves*!

They helped themselves. – Sie haben sich beide selbst bedient.
They helped each other. – Sie haben einander geholfen.

15 Sieh dir die Bilder an und vervollständige die Sätze mit *each other* oder *themselves*.

1. They met _____.

2. They looked at _____.

3. They looked at _____.

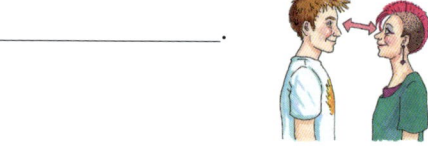

4. They taught _____ to build a boat.

5. They took photos of _____.

Wiederholung: Bedingungssätze – Typ 1

Wenn etwas passieren **könnte** und du sagen willst, was dann passiert, verwendest du den Typ-1-Bedingungssatz.

Bedingung im *if*-Satz *simple present*	Folge im Hauptsatz *will future*
If it rains later, If John and I meet today, If Mike doesn't come to my party,	I'll stay at home. we'll watch a film together. I won't be happy.

Wenn man den Hauptsatz zuerst nennt, verwendet man kein Komma.

What will you do if it your dad doesn't give you any money?
I won't be able to buy anything if I don't get any money.

16 Meine Schwester. Verwende die angegebenen Wörter, um vollständige Typ-1-Bedingungssätze zu bilden.

if – my sister's boyfriend – to ask – her – she – to marry – him

_____

my dad – not – to be happy – if – she – to marry – him – soon

_____

if – they – to marry – my sister – to leave – home

_____

if – my sister – to leave – home – I – to have – my own room. Hurray.

_____

I – to be – happy – if – I – to have – my own room – ?

_____

Bedingungssätze – Typ 2

> Du verwendest Typ-2-Bedingungssätze, wenn
>
> – etwas sehr **unwahrscheinlich** erscheint:
> If I won one million pounds, I would never have to work. – Wenn ich eine Million Pfund gewinnen würde, müsste ich niemals arbeiten.
>
> – oder **unmöglich** ist:
> I'd live in a palace if I was queen. – Ich würde in einem Palast leben, wenn ich Königin wäre.
>
> | Bedingung im *if*-Satz
simple past | Folge im Hauptsatz
would + Infinitiv |
> |---|---|
> | If there was no school today,
If I didn't have a sister,
If I couldn't go to school, | I'd go swimming.
I could have my own room.
I wouldn't be happy. |
>
> Statt *would* + Infinitiv kannst du auch *could* oder *might* + Infinitiv im Hauptsatz verwenden.
>
> Wenn du jemandem einen Rat geben willst, kannst du sagen: *If I were you* oder *If I was you*: If I were you, I wouldn't do that.

17 Wenn mein Vater reich wäre … Ergänze die richtige Form der Verben.

If my dad _____ (be) rich, we could live in a big house.

If we lived in a big house with a garden, I _____ (have)

my own horse. If our house _____ (have) lots of rooms,

I _____ (needn't) share a room with my sister.

I _____ (buy) more clothes if I had more money. If my

dad was rich, my parents _____ (needn't) work.

If my parents _____ (not/work), they might stay at home

all day. Yuk! I'm glad my dad isn't rich.

18 Geburtstag. Verbinde die Satzhälften sinnvoll miteinander.

I'll have my party at my sport's club	will he bring his friends?
If I invite all my friends,	if I could cook well.
If we had a big house,	I'll save it for a holiday.
We could have a party in the garden	all my friends could come here.
If my dad gives me money,	will they all come?
I'd make a cake	if they let me.
If I ask my brother,	if my birthday was in summer.

19 Ergänze die angegebenen Verben in den richtigen Formen.

Our house is small. If we _____ (have) more rooms, I think we _____ (fight) less. For example, we _____ (not/have) the same problems in the morning if we _____ (have) more bathrooms. My brother is 18 soon and he wants to go to Spain for a year. If he _____ (go) to Spain, we _____ (have) more room at home, but I _____ (miss) him. If he _____ (like) it, he _____ (may) stay there. If he _____ (stay) there, maybe I _____ (can) stay with him but maybe he _____ (not/invite) me. If we all _____ (live) in Spain, we _____ _____ (not/need) a big house because we _____ (can) live outside more. I'd like that.

Bedingungssätze – Typ 3

Du verwendest Typ-3-Bedingungssätze, wenn du über ein **vergangenes** Ereignis sprichst, das **nicht eingetreten** ist bzw. nicht mehr eintreten kann.

If I **hadn't had** my party at home, I **would have invited** more friends. – Wenn ich mein Fest nicht zuhause veranstaltet hätte, hätte ich mehr Freunde eingeladen (das war aber nicht so).

Bedingung im *if*-Satz past perfect	Folge im Hauptsatz conditional perfect (would + have + past participle)
If you hadn't eaten too much, If I hadn't missed the bus, If she had had more money,	you wouldn't have felt ill. I wouldn't have been late. she could have bought more.

Statt *would + have + past participle* kannst du auch *could* oder *might + have + past participle* im Hauptsatz verwenden.

Achtung bei den Kurzformen: **'d** kann *would* oder *had* bedeuten!

If I**'d** had more time, I**'d** have eaten more. = If I **had** had more time, I **would** have eaten more.

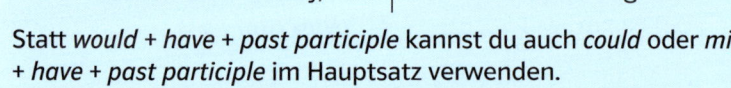

20 Letztes Wochenende. Bilde aus den Satzteilen Bedingungssätze vom Typ 3.

if – I – not – to watch the late film – I – to get up earlier

_____

if – I – to get up earlier – I – to go – to London – with my friends

_____

if – I – to go – to London – I – to meet – my favourite actor, too

_____

he – might – to speak – to me – if – I – to meet him

_____

21 Ein Abend und seine Folgen. Welcher *if*-Satz-Typ ist gefragt? Trage die richtigen Verbformen ein.

My parents went out last night. If my parents _____ (not/go) out, I _____ (not/invite) my friends. Joanne's cousins were staying with her over the weekend. If they _____ (not/be) at her house, she _____ (not/bring) them with her. If she _____ (not/bring) her cousins, they _____ (cannot/break) my mum's favourite clock. It's Sunday today. If it _____ (be) Saturday, I _____ (to look for) a new clock for my mother. I've got an idea: I could try to mend it. If I mend it well, she _____ (not/know) that they broke it – maybe. Oh no. They're coming. I know, if I _____ (hide) it, she _____ (not/see) it and I'll be able to buy a new one tomorrow. What a pain! If my parents _____ (go out) next weekend, I _____ (stay) at home alone!

Tipp → Erinnere dich: Nur wenn der Bedingungssatz zuerst kommt, setzt du ein Komma!

22 Übersetze.

Das Theaterstück wäre nicht so gut gewesen, wenn du nicht hart gearbeitet hättest. Wenn ich du wäre, würde ich für ein weiteres Theaterstück vorsprechen.

_____

_____

Ein Theaterstück

23 Lies den Text einmal durch und ordne dann die Szenenanweisungen den richtigen Szenen zu.

Scene 1
Chris: Hey, what do you think about these?
Sue: Well, they're nice, but I always wear trousers. I'd really like to buy a new skirt for my birthday party. A short one.
Chris: If you buy a very short one, your mum will never let you wear it.
Sue: Yeah, I know. Well, it doesn't have to be that short.
Chris: What about this dress? You'd look good in this.
Sue: Yeah, that's really cool, and I'd get it if I had more money. But have you seen the price?
Chris: Oh yeah.
Sue: I'd like to try these skirts on but where's the assistant?
Chris: Er. Hey, isn't that your boyfriend over there?
Sue: Where? Where? Oh, yeah. Oh, and look. He's with Jane.
Chris: Oh yeah. I didn't see her.
Sue: What are they doing together?
Chris: Er …
Sue: Look at them. They're having a great time together. Look! He's got his arm on her shoulders. Oh no!
Chris: Hey Sue. Sue, come back. Oh no.

Scene 2
Mum: Sue, do you want something to eat?
Sue: No, I'm not hungry.
Mum: Oh Sue. You must eat something. You haven't eaten all day. Oh, there's the phone again. Sue, you answer it. It's probably Jane again. She's already tried to phone you three times.
Sue: I don't want to talk to her.
Mum: Why not? What's happened? She's one of your best friends.
Sue: No, she isn't. If she'd been my friend, she wouldn't have gone out with my boyfriend.
Mum: What do you mean?
Sue: I saw her yesterday in town. And she was with Steve. They were both laughing and really enjoying themselves. They weren't thinking about me. That was clear.
Mum: Maybe it wasn't how you thought. If you spoke to her, you'd find out.

Scene 3
(You can't see Mum but you can hear her voice)
Mum: Hi Jane. Come in. She's just in there.
Jane: Hi Sue. Happy Birthday.
Sue: (in grumpy voice) I don't want to talk to you.
Jane: Oh Sue. Chris has told me why you're angry. You saw me and Steve together in town, didn't you?

Sue:	Yes. Oh Jane. How could you do it? I thought you were my friend.
Jane:	*(shouting)* Yes, I am. And if you thought well of me, you would know that I would never go out with your boyfriend.
Sue:	*(angrily)* I never thought you would. But you have to believe your eyes, don't you?
Jane:	Yes, but what did you see? You saw me and Steve in your favourite shop, didn't you? Do you think I'm so stupid? If I had wanted to go out with your boyfriend, I wouldn't have gone to your favourite shop. Would I? Use your head. What do you think we were doing in your favourite shop just before your birthday?
Sue:	*(embarrassed)* Er … You weren't … er …
Jane:	Yes, I was. I was helping Steve to find a present for you.
Sue:	Oh no. Have you told Steve?
Jane:	No, if you want to tell him about your mistake, you'll have to tell him yourself.

Instructions for the scene:
a) At home. Sue is sitting in an armchair and she's watching TV. Her mum is standing near the door.
b) At home. Sue is sitting in an armchair and she's watching TV. She's wearing different clothes and she's just got up. Somebody has just knocked at the door.
c) In a shop. They're looking at clothes. It's Saturday and there are lots of other people there.

Scene 1: _____   Scene 2: _____   Scence 3: _____

24 Fragen zum Text in Übung 23. Wähle die richtige Antwort.

1. What did Sue want to buy in the shop?
   a) a dress ☐
   b) a skirt ☐
   c) trousers ☐

2. Why didn't Sue want to buy the dress?
   a) It was too expensive. ☐
   b) She didn't want a dress. ☐
   c) She liked trousers better. ☐

| 3 | Wortschatz | Grammatik | **Leseverstehen** | Hörverstehen |

3. Who was Sue's boyfriend with? a) Jane ☐, b) Sue ☐, c) Chris ☐

4. Sue doesn't want to talk to Jane
   because Jane …
   a) called her too often. ☐
   b) was in her favourite shop. ☐
   c) went out with Steve. ☐

5. Jane was in the shop because
   she was …
   a) looking for a dress. ☐
   b) helping Steve buy a present. ☐
   c) looking for clothes for Steve. ☐

6. Does Steve know that Sue
   was angry? a) Not in the text. ☐ b) Yes. ☐ c) No. ☐

25 Wie sind diese Bedingungssätze gemeint? Wähle den entsprechenden Satz.

1. "If you buy a very short one, your mum will never let you wear it."
a) Sue may buy one.
b) Sue won't buy one.
c) Sue has already bought one. → Satz _____

2. "I'd get it if I had more money."
a) She may have more money.
b) She hasn't got enough money.
c) She had enough money in the past. → Satz _____

3. "If I had wanted to go out with your boyfriend, I wouldn't have gone to your favourite shop."
a) Jane may want to go out with Sue's boyfriend.
b) Jane doesn't want to go out with Sue's boyfriend.
c) Jane didn't want to go out with Sue's boyfriend in the past. → Satz _____

4. "… if you want to tell him about your mistake, you'll have to tell him yourself."
a) Sue may want to tell him.
b) Sue doesn't want to tell him.
c) Sue wanted to tell him in the past. → Satz _____

Zuhören: *Wordstress* 💿 12

26 Höre dir den CD-Track an und ordne die Wörter der richtigen Spalte zu. Auf welcher Silbe (großes X) werden die Wörter betont?

answerphone   behave   decide   decision   especially   frozen

marry   microwave   myself   probably   reflexive   selfish

xX	Xx	xXx	Xxx
____	____	____	____
____	____	____	____
____	____	____	____

Tipp: Sprich die Wörter laut aus – es hilft! Achte besonders auf die Wörter, die im Englischen und Deutschen gleich geschrieben werden, aber unterschiedlich betont werden wie „Moment" oder „modern".

Zuhören und das Wesentliche verstehen 💿 13

27 Ein Streit. Höre dir den Dialog auf der CD an, dann verbinde die Sätze so, wie sie im Text vorkommen.

Can we talk	you'd be home at 10 o'clock.
We agreed that	if do all your homework first.
I know, but	I was very worried about you last night.
Well, you've got a point, but	but can't we meet halfway?
I guess you're right	about last night?
I'll let you stay out later on Saturday	I'm not your friends' mum.

Hörverstehen: Telefongespräche

Am Telefon ist es meist schwieriger, jemanden zu verstehen, weil man die Person nicht sieht. Mit etwas Übung wird es besser gehen, du kannst aber auch folgende Tipps beherzigen, um es dir leichter zu machen.

Wenn du direkt mit jemandem sprichst:
– Bitte deine/-n Gesprächspartner/-in zu wiederholen, was er/sie sagt, wenn du ihn/sie nicht verstanden hast.
– Wiederhole selbst, was du gehört hast, um sicherzustellen, dass du alles richtig verstanden hast.

Wenn du eine Nachricht auf dem AB abhörst:
– Höre dir die Nachricht so oft an, bis du sie verstehst.
– Mach dir Notizen.

Zuhören: Drei Telefongespräche 14

28 Hör dir den CD-Track an und beantworte zu jedem Gespräch die Fragen. Höre dir die Dialoge so oft an, wie du willst!

Phone call 1:

a) Who does Kylie want to speak to? _____

b) Where is she? _____

c) What does Kylie want Ann to do? _____

Phone call 2:

a) Who's calling? _____

b) Why is she calling? _____

c) When does she want her friend to call back? _____

Phone call 3:

a) Who is calling? _____

b) What's his phone number? _____

c) What should Neil's dad do? _____

Unit 4

Der Nordwesten Englands

1 Ergänze die Lücken mit den passenden Wörtern.

coal mines – facelift – firms – heavy industry – landscape – industry – leisure – region – waterfront

The northwest of England is famous for its _____ – the Industrial Revolution started here – but it is also a beautiful _____. Away from the cities the _____ is wild with many mountains and lakes and it's perfect for many _____ activities like rock climbing. Even the cities are beautiful and interesting. Manchester has had a _____ recently and Liverpool's _____ is a must-see. Around the area you can still see lots of signs of the _____ which was once so important here, for example, you can still see _____ although they are not used any more. Now many new smaller _____ have started in the area; more people work in high-tech or leisure industries now. The area has changed and left its past behind.

Nationalitäten

2 Nenne zu den Orten jeweils die Nationalität bzw. das Adjektiv.

Wales _____ Scotland _____ Punjab _____

Italy _____ Asia _____ America _____

Verben

3 Die Sinne. Übersetze die gefragten Verben.

1. riechen _____   2. duften _____

klingen _____   hören _____

aussehen _____   schauen _____

fühlen _____   sich anfühlen _____

schmecken _____   scheinen _____

4 Löse die Anagramme auf und ordne die Verben den richtigen Sätzen zu.

I'd love to _____ those new skateparks. | ceehrde

A skater did a great trick and everybody _____. | sexits

We're going to _____ to Cardiff. | voem

Not much heavy industry _____ there now. | tyr tou

5 Welche Präpositionen fehlen hier? Ergänze.

My cousin is very proud _____ his job. He helps bands at their shows

and he's always _____ the move. He's really _____ music

so he loves it and although he has to work really hard, he never gets

tired _____ it. We always make fun _____ him because he often

hangs _____ with these famous people, but he doesn't mind – he

wants to be in a band, too, one day.

Wortgitter

6 Suche die zehn Wörter aus den Wortfeldern Essen, Menschen und Orte, die sich in dem Wortgitter verbergen, und ordne sie zu.

d	t	a	s	t	e	q	m	e	f
c	g	p	r	e	g	i	o	n	e
r	b	h	r	j	z	n	t	v	n
o	a	l	e	r	n	a	o	o	g
w	n	c	l	a	f	x	r	z	i
d	l	u	a	s	h	r	w	l	n
b	i	r	t	h	p	l	a	c	e
w	k	r	i	d	g	u	y	k	e
a	x	y	v	f	u	s	b	o	r
t	e	a	e	d	i	n	n	e	r

food	_____
people	_____
places	_____

Adjektive

7 Suche aus der Buchstabenschlange fünf Adjektive heraus und schreibe sie neben das passende Substantiv.

abstractbilingualdefiniteregionalweird

_____ culture   _____ children

_____ noun   _____ place

_____ article

69

by/until

8 Ergänze: Musst du *by* oder *until* in die Lücken eintragen?

1. We need to be at the theatre _____ 8 pm. If we're there later, they won't let us in.

2. I think you can buy tickets _____ 7.30, but not later.

3. The play won't start _____ 8.15. It won't start before then.

Wichtige Wendungen: Jemandem helfen/sich entschuldigen

9 Bilde aus den angegebenen Wörtern Sätze und trage sie richtig ein.

> more/well,/be/next/time/careful   very/of/that's/you/kind
>
> to/I/rude/didn't/be/mean   help/you/can/I

Man: Are you lost? _____?

Woman: Yes please. Can you tell me how to get to the waterfront museum?

Man: Yes, I can show you the way if you like.

Woman: _____

Girl: I'm terrible sorry if I hurt you yesterday.

Mum: Yes, you did. Never mind if that's what you think.

Girl: _____

Mum: _____

Wiederholung: Adjektiv oder Adverb?

> Du verwendest **Adverbien**, um auszudrücken, wie jemand etwas *macht*. Mit **Adjektiven** beschreibst du, wie etwas *ist*.
> He **drives badly.** He's a **bad driver.**
> Adverbien stehen meistens nach dem Objekt.
> He eats **curry quickly.**
> Du bildest die meisten Adverbien, indem du an das Adjektiv **-ly** hängst. Achte auf folgende Schreibregeln:
>
> | Adjektiv | Adverb | |
> | --- | --- | --- |
> | weird | **weirdly** | + -ly |
> | awful | **awfully** | -ful → -fully |
> | crazy | **crazily** | -y nach Konsonant → -ily |
> | horrible | **horribly** | -le → -ily |
>
> Daneben gibt es ein paar Ausnahmen, die du auswendig lernen musst.
> He sings **well** but he speaks **fast**. He tries **hard** and he talks in a **friendly way.**

10 Ergänze die angegebenen Wörter in der richtigen Form: Brauchst du das Adjektiv oder das Adverb? Manche benötigst du zweimal!

beautiful – friendly – hard – strange

I've just moved to Wales and I love it here. It's a _____ place – the mountains and the coastline are lovely – and the people are _____. Most people here speak English and Welsh and I want to learn Welsh, too, although I think it's a _____ language. Maybe if I work _____, I'll be able to understand people soon. When they speak English, they have _____ accents but I think they speak _____. It sounds like the people are singing. And many people sing well, too, although not everybody is in a choir, of course.

Wiederholung: Possessivpronomen

possessive determiners + nouns	possessive pronouns
That's **my** soup.	And that drink is **mine**, too.
Is this **your** book?	Or is that **yours**?
Have you got **his** bag, too?	No, **his** is in the house.
Is that **her** cat?	Yes, and the dog is **hers**, too.
Great. Here is **our** train.	No, that's not **ours**.
Boys, have you got **your** books?	And girls, have you got **yours**, too?
Is that **their** house?	No, **theirs** is number 12.

11 Im Zug. Ergänze jeweils Possessivpronomen bzw. Possessivbegleiter.

Sue: Is that our carriage?

John: Er … let me just look at _____ tickets. Er … No, it isn't _____. We need number 14.

(…)

Man: Excuse me. I think you are sitting in _____ seat.

John: No, I'm sure it's _____. Look! Here's _____ ticket. Can I see _____ ticket, please?

Man: Yes, here it is. Look. Seat 56, carriage 13.

John: Oh, but this is carriage 14. _____ must be the next one.

(…)

Sue: What a funny day! Look that boy can't find _____ seat now.

John: The seat opposite us is empty. Maybe that's _____.

Sue: No, that seat is that girl's. Look! That coat is _____.

John: Oh yes. Why can't people find _____ seats easily!

Der bestimmte Artikel

> Du verwendest den bestimmten Artikel, wenn du über etwas Bestimmtes redest: I love **the book** which I'm reading at the moment.
>
> Keinen Artikel verwendest du, wenn du über Menschen oder Sachen im Allgemeinen sprichst: I love **books.**
>
> Es existieren allerdings einige Substantive, bei denen es Unterschiede zum Deutschen gibt.
>
> – abstrakte Begriffe (z. B. *money, time, life, love, work, school*):
>
> | | |
> |---|---|
> | I love **school.** (allgemein) *aber:* I don't like the school which I go to. (eine bestimmte Schule) | … die Schule. |
>
> – Verkehrsmittel:
>
> | | |
> |---|---|
> | My mum goes to work **by boat.** *aber:* The boat which took us to England was small. | … mit dem Boot. |
>
> – Mahlzeiten:
>
> | | |
> |---|---|
> | We usually eat **tea** about 6 o'clock. *aber:* The tea we eat today was delicious. | … das Abendessen … |

12 Übersetze.

Macht dich Geld glücklich?

Does _____ happy?

Fährst du mit dem Fahrrad zur Schule?

Do you _____ bike?

Ich liebe Musik.

I _____ music.

Meine Eltern mögen nicht die Musik, die ich mag.

My parents don't _____ which I like.

Der unbestimmte Artikel

Den unbestimmten Artikel verwendest du, wenn du über etwas Unbestimmtes redest (wie im Deutschen): I'd like **a biscuit**.
Einige Unterschiede gibt es jedoch:

– Berufszeichnungen:
My mum's **an engineer**. | Meine Mutter ist **Ingenieurin**.

– Redewendungen:
Is she **in a hurry**? | Ist sie **in Eile**?
I've got **a headache**. | Ich habe **Kopfschmerzen**.

13 Entscheide: Artikel oder nicht, bestimmter oder unbestimmter Artikel? Ergänze die Lücken richtig.

I like _____ school really but I don't feel so good today and _____ school which I go to is on the other side of town so I really don't want to go today. I usually go by _____ bus, of course and I can't come home for _____ lunch, but that's no problem.

I've got _____ headache, but I don't need to see _____ doctor because my mum's _____ doctor. She says that I'm not ill and I have to go to _____ school. She says I just stayed out too late last night. My mum never lets me stay at home. I wish she was _____ engineer or something and then I could see _____ normal doctor.

I went to see _____ band last night. _____ music wasn't very good but _____ singer was wonderful. He's _____ love of my life – well, at _____ moment anyway. I don't need _____ boyfriend but _____ love makes _____ life sweeter, doesn't it? And I love _____ music so it's great to have _____ boyfriend who can sing well.

Das Adjektiv als Substantiv

> In Englischen kannst du ein Adjektiv nur in bestimmten Fällen als Substantiv verwenden: wenn es sich auf eine ganze Gruppe von Menschen bezieht.
>
> Life is hard for **the poor.** (= die Armen generell)
>
> Are **the famous** always rich? (= alle berühmten Leute)
>
> Das Substantiv wird als Pluralform behandelt, obwohl es keine Pluralendung hat:
>
> **Are the good** happier than the bad? – Yes, **they are.**
>
> Wenn man einzelne Personen oder bestimmte Gruppen meint, brauchst man ein Substantiv bzw. das Stützwort *one/ones*:
>
> **Rich men** are usually healthier than **poor ones.**

14 Ersetze die Kombination Adjektiv + Substantiv durch ein Pluralform-Substantiv, wo es möglich ist.

1. Rich people aren't always happier than poor people.
2. Rich women don't always dress better than poor women.
3. That blind girl goes to our school.
4. She doesn't go to a school for blind people.
5. Are old men and women usually wise?
6. Young children learn best from older children.

Adjektive nach bestimmten Verben

> **Adverbien** beschreiben, wie sich etwas verhält. Sie stehen üblicherweise **nach dem Verb:**
>
> We go in quickly when it rains heavily.
>
> **Adjektive** sagen aus, wie etwas ist. Sie stehen normalerweise **vor dem Substantiv** oder **nach *to be*:**
>
> They're nice people and their house is interesting.
>
> Einige Verben jedoch, die einen **Zustand** beschreiben, benötigen Adjektive und nicht Adverbien. Zu ihnen gehören:
>
> – *be, seem, feel, stay* (Zustand/Eigenschaft):
>
> She **seems clever** but I don't know her well.
> This bag **stays cold** even when it's warm.
>
> – *become, get* („werden"):
>
> It's **getting warm**, isn't it?
>
> – *look, smell, sound, taste, feel* (Sinneswahrnehmung):
>
> That food **looks good** and it **smells delicious.**
>
> Aber: Wenn man *look, smell, feel* oder *taste* dazu verwendet auszudrücken, *wie* man die Aktion *macht*, steht das Adverb:
>
> I **looked** at my book **quickly.**

15 Lies den Text. Unterstreiche die normalen Adjektive einfach, die Zustandsadjektive zweifach und unterstrichele die Adverbien.

My aunt's got a good job but it isn't always easy. She works hard and for many hours and so she often gets tired. She works with young people so it's good that she's a friendly person. Sometimes people react badly or shout at her angrily but she always stays calm. She likes people and gets on well with most people so she usually feels good about her job. And what is it? She's a teacher.

16 Essengehen in Canterbury. Entscheide dich: Adjektiv oder Adverb? Unterstreiche das richtige Wort.

Maria went to Canterbury to learn English. She arrived on Friday evening and walked slow/slowly around the town. She thought that it looked beautiful/beautifully. Many of the buildings were old/oldly and there were lots of interesting/interestingly restaurants and theatres, too. After some time she got hungry/hungrily and decided to try some good/well English food. The first restaurant she found smelt delicious/deliciously but it was French. She found five more restaurants quick/quickly but not one of them was English. She asked somebody but she didn't understand the answer because the woman's English sounded strange/strangely. She was Italian. Then she heard some music in one restaurant and people were talking happy/happily. It sounded and smelt great/greatly and so she went in. It was Irish.

17 Bilde mit den angegebenen Wörtern eine Mindmap. Achtung: Brauchst du die Adjektiv- oder die Adverbform?

fast
dangerous
good
interesting
young
happy

Das Futur II

> Du verwendest das *future perfect*, wenn du sagen willst, dass etwas bis zu einem bestimmten Zeitpunkt in der Zukunft abgeschlossen sein wird.
>
> I **will have arrived** by 10 o'clock tomorrow. – Ich werde morgen bis 10 Uhr angekommen sein.
>
> She **won't have finished** her homework before our next lesson. – Sie wird ihre Hausaufgaben nicht vor unserer nächsten Stunde gemacht haben.
>
> What **will** you **have done** by Sunday evening? – Was wirst du bis Sonntagabend erledigt haben?
>
> Du bildest das *future perfect* mit **will/won't + have + past participle**. Die Form ist für alle Personen gleich.

18 Ferien. Bilde mithilfe der Wörter Sätze mit dem *future perfect*.

I – forget – everything – I learned – at school – by Monday morning

_____

my older brother – leave England – by Sunday night

_____

I – fight – with my sister – before the end of the weekend

_____

I – not – do – any schoolwork – by the last day of the holidays

_____

we – all – swim – in the sea

_____

we – not – get bored – before the end of the holidays

_____

Grammatik 4

19 Zeitformen der Zukunft: Wann verwendest du welche? Lies die Sätze und überlege, für welchen Sachverhalt du welche Zeit benötigst.

a) You want to do something next year.
b) You're talking about a time on a timetable.
c) You've made an arrangement to meet somebody tomorrow.
d) You decide something spontaneously.
e) You want to say how old you are on your next birthday.
f) You know that something is going to happen before a certain time in the future.
g) You can see something now that tells you about the future.

simple present: _____   *going to future:* _____

present progressive: _____   *future perfect:* _____

will future: _____

20 Ein Umzug. Unterstreiche die richtige Form der Zukunft.

A friend is moving/will move house tomorrow. Her train leaves/is going to leave at 11 o'clock and I'm going/'ll go to the station with her. Her dad is going to travel/travels down with all their things the day after. By this time next week she'll have started/'ll start her new school and she'll have made/'s making some new friends.

She doesn't want to leave. She says things are worse for her than for me because she won't/isn't going to know anybody there and she'll miss/is missing everything here. I think she's wrong. Things will be/are going to be worse for me. Everything will be/is going to be exciting for her. I'll have visited/'m going to visit her at Christmas and by then she meets/'ll have met lots of new people and done lots of new things. I'm not doing/won't have done anything new. There'll just be a hole where she was.

Paarwörter

Trousers, jeans, glasses sind Paarwörter, weil sie aus zwei Teilen bestehen (z. B. zwei Brillengläser). Deshalb spricht man von ihnen immer im Plural.

I like your new **trousers. They**'re very nice.
I've lost my **glasses.** Have you seen **them?**

Wenn du sagen willst, wie viele von ihnen du hast, verwendest du *a pair of.*

I've got **two pairs of shoes.**
She's got **a new pair of glasses.**

21 Sieh dir die Bilder an und schreibe die richtigen Wörter in die Lücken.

1. I'm glad, I needn't wear _____. They're very expensive. My mum's got three _____ and she loses _____ all the time.

2. I don't wear _____ very often. I don't like them. I've only got two _____.

3. I love _____. I've got 15 _____ _____. I even wear _____ at school.

4. My friend loves _____. She's just bought three _____. She works so that she can buy new _____.

Reading skills: Sachtexte

> Wenn du nach bestimmten Informationen suchst, also z. B. an einem Projekt arbeitest oder ein passendes Urlaubsziel ausfindig machen möchtest, liest du Sachtexte *(factual texts)*. Um festzustellen, ob und wie sie dir hilfreich sein können, gibt es zwei Methoden.
>
> *Skimming* **(Überfliegen):**
> Zunächst überfliegst du den Text nur, denn du willst nur ungefähr wissen, wovon der Text handelt. Außerdem muss es schnell gehen, denn vielleicht ist der Text für dich gar nicht interessant. Achte nur auf Schlüsselwörter, z. B. Verben und Substantive.
>
> *Scanning* **(Durchsuchen nach Details):**
> Wenn du den richtigen Text gefunden hast, suchst du gezielt nach bestimmten Informationen. Du überfliegst also den Text ein zweites Mal, aber diesmal fahndest du ganz konkret nach bestimmten Wörtern.

22 William, Ellen, Maria und Liam möchten in Großbritannien Urlaub machen. „Skimme" die Texte und wähle aus, welche beiden Orte jeweils für welche Person interessant sein könnten.

William wants to walk in the country. He likes the water. _____

Ellen wants to go on a short break to a city. _____

Maria likes the country and wants to relax. _____

Liam wants to visit a city and the country. _____

A: Isle of Wight
The Isle of Wight is a small island off the south coast of England. The two biggest towns on the island are Newport, its capital, and Ryde, where most people arrive by boat. There are also many smaller villages around the island, most of them on the coast. The Isle of Wight has not changed a lot in the last fifty years and it is an ideal place for people who like to enjoy life slowly and for people who love the sea and walks in beautiful country.

There are beautiful beaches all around the island but they are different on the different coasts. If you enjoy surfing or windsurfing and big waves, try the west of the island. If you like empty beaches to enjoy by yourself, try the south of the island. The best place for sailing is Cowes on the north coast. The Isle of Wight has no mountains but it is a hilly place and a great place to cycle and walk. The weather also helps as the Isle of Wight is one of the sunniest places in Great Britain.

There are also many interesting places to visit on the Isle of Wight. You can visit many historical places such as castles and Roman ruins. Or try a theme park, the zoo or one of the many museums here.

B: Newcastle

Many tourists to England don't get as far north as Newcastle – and they miss a lot. Newcastle has a lot to offer but what it is probably most famous for is its nightlife. It has maybe the best nightlife in England. It is a small city and so it's easy to visit a lot of places in a short time. There are many theatres, nightclubs, discos, bars and restaurants. There is something for anybody who likes to go out in the evening or who likes music. Try one of the nightclubs by the river and if you go at the right time of year, you can also go to one of the many festivals in Newcastle. But don't take a coat with you or you'll look like a tourist – even in winter "Geordies" (the local people from Newcastle) usually go out just in shirts or dresses.

It is not only the nightlife which is interesting: Newcastle is great for shopping, too. It also has many museums, art galleries, historically interesting places and its football club. The football club is important in Newcastle. Many Geordies love football and on Saturdays you don't need to see the score to know if Newcastle has won or not. If you want to get out of the city for a day, there are many interesting and beautiful places to choose from. Newcastle is near the coast and so for anybody who is interested in water sports, it is a great place to visit. There are also some great country parks nearby for people who like a walk in the country.

C: The Lake District

The Lake District is in the northwest of England. As you can see by the name, there are many lakes here and there are also many mountains. The Lake District is very popular with British walkers and climbers; the sporty and the not-so-sporty. You could spend years walking in the Lake District and not have to walk on the same path twice. The not-so-sporty can walk around lakes, have tea and return by boat.

The Lake District is also by the coast and so it is an interesting place for people who like water sports of any kind. You can canoe or sail in the sea, the rivers or in the lakes here. You can swim or dive. And if you don't like sport at all, you can just sit and enjoy the beautiful views. The Lake District is mostly famous because the country is so wild and beautiful. Many English poets came here in the nineteenth century to write, and many people also come to visit the places that they wrote about or the places they wrote.

There are no very big towns in the Lake District, and although there are interesting places here to visit, it is really a place for people who love to be outside. And for people who don't mind the rain: the Lake District is one of the wettest places in Great Britain.

D: Bristol

Bristol is a very interesting city historically and was one of England's biggest cities until the Industrial Revolution. The Romans settled here and you can still see Roman ruins here or at the nearby town, Bath. Later Bristol, which is in the west of England, became an important harbour as people started to sail to America.

Bristol is a very attractive city and a place which is easy to enjoy. The River Avon runs through the middle and you can go on boat trips through the city and out into the country. There are lots of things to do in Bristol – places to visit, museums, sport, shopping, theatres, cinemas – but it is also a place where you can just sit and relax. It has a good nightlife, too, and Bristol is famous for its music and film industries.

Bristol is also a perfect place from which to visit South Wales and Cornwall, Devon and Dorset. You can go by rail, by car or bus and visit many interesting places for the day. For anybody who is coming from a different country, Bristol is easy to get to, by train or by plane.

4 | Wortschatz | Grammatik | **Leseverstehen** | Hörverstehen

23 Lies weitere Informationen über William, Ellen, Maria und Liam. Dann „scanne" die Texte, die du in Übung 22 jeweils ausgesucht hattest, und überlege, welcher von beiden gewählten Orten eher die Interessen abdeckt: Welcher Urlaubsort ist am geeignetsten?

William loves …
- mountains
- sailing
- canoeing
- the sea

→ _____

Maria loves …
- mountains
- surfing
- historical places
- the sea

→ _____

Ellen loves …
- music
- films
- Roman ruins
- shopping

→ _____

Liam loves …
- music
- nightclubs
- football
- the sea

_____

24 Lies den Text in Übung 22 nochmals und beantworte dann die Fragen dazu.

1. Where is the Isle of Wight? _____

2. How much has it changed in the last 50 years? _____

3. What can you do in the west of the island? _____

4. Where's Newcastle? _____

5. What's Newcastle most famous for? _____

6. What do many Geordies love? _____

7. Where's the Lake District? _____

8. What can you do there? _____

9. What's the weather like? _____

10. Which places are easy to visit from Bristol? _____

11. What is Bristol famous for? _____

12. Where did people sail to from Bristol? _____

25 Sind die Aussagen *true, false* oder *not in the text?* Korrigiere dann die Sätze, die falsch sind.

	true	false	not in the text
1. There are many hills on the Isle of Wight.	☐	☐	☐
2. It doesn't rain much on the Isle of Wight.	☐	☐	☐
3. Many tourists visit Newcastle.	☐	☐	☐
4. A river runs through Newcastle.	☐	☐	☐
5. You have to be very fit to walk in the Lake District.	☐	☐	☐
6. You can swim in all the lakes in the Lake District.	☐	☐	☐
7. Bristol doesn't have an airport.	☐	☐	☐

Korrektur: _____

Zuhören: Aussprache 15

26 Lies dir erst die Wörter durch, dann höre dir den CD-Track an. Welches Wort wird gesprochen?

1. weird	☐	we'd ☐
2. quite	☐	quiet ☐
3. smelled	☐	smelt ☐
4. eyes	☐	ice ☐
5. hat	☐	head ☐

Zuhören und richtig reagieren 16

27 Du hörst drei Kurzdialoge, in denen jeweils eine Zeile fehlt *(part 1)*. Welche Zeile fehlt? Wähle die beste Antwort. Höre dann *part 2* der Lösung an und prüfe, ob du recht hattest.

1. a) You've been a great help. ☐
   b) That's very kind of you. Thanks. ☐
   c) Don't worry. ☐

2. a) Do you live near here? ☐
   b) Just take your time. ☐
   c) Haven't we met before? ☐

3. a) Don't worry. ☐
   b) I didn't mean to be rude. ☐
   c) That's very kind of you. ☐

Hörverstehen 4

Zuhören: Ein Umzug 🎧 17

28 Höre dir das Telefongespräch an, dann entscheide dich: Welche Beschreibung passt am besten?

a) Luke has moved house and is talking to his friend Lisa on the phone. ☐

b) Luke is going to move house and has just been to visit their new house. ☐

c) Luke is going on holiday for the whole summer. ☐

Tipp → Du brauchst nicht jedes Wort zu verstehen, um den Sinn einer Unterhaltung zu erfassen. Wenn du bestimmte Informationen suchst, konzentriere dich auf die relevanten Wörter.

29 Lies zunächst die Fragen durch, dann höre dir den CD-Track nochmals an. Welche Antwort ist richtig?

1. Where's Luke going to move to?

a) Brighton ☐
b) Bristol ☐
c) Birmingham ☐

2. Where are they going to live?

a) in the country ☐
b) on a hill ☐
c) near the sea ☐

3. When are they going to move?

a) the end of June ☐
b) the end of July ☐
c) the end of August ☐

4. Who's Luke meeting on his birthday?

a) Jill ☐
b) friends from his old school ☐
c) friends from his new school ☐

5. When will Luke forget Jill?

a) at Christmas ☐
b) before Christmas ☐
c) after Christmas ☐

Revision B (Unit 3–4)

Go, get, make oder take?

1 Übersetze. Welches Substantiv erfordert welches Verb?

ein Risiko eingehen   _____

sich anziehen   _____

sich kräuseln   _____

eine Entscheidung treffen   _____

sichergehen   _____

ausflippen   _____

sich Zeit lassen   _____

sich lustig machen über   _____

etwas sattbekommen   _____

Zwei-Wort-Verben

2 Ergänze die Lücken mit den fehlenden Präpositionen.

Caroline won't go _____ with me and I don't know why. Don't you feel sorry _____ me? I'm a really nice guy. I eat _____ my vegetables, turn _____ my mp3 player when teachers are talking and I get _____ with everybody – well, almost. I'm _____ books, music and sport. I'm good _____ school and my parents are proud _____ me. I don't hang _____ with the wrong people. I don't make fun _____ people and I never laugh _____ rude jokes. Well, maybe I'm just too perfect!

Odd one out

3 Finde jeweils die Person bzw. Sache, die nicht in die Reihe passt.

1.
cleaning lady
witch
guy
actress
→ _____

2.
audience
crowd
male voice choir
caller
→ _____

3.
vegetarian
engineer
cleaning lady
director
→ _____

4.
tea
purse
curry
crust
→ _____

5.
doorbell
telephone
answerphone
junk
→ _____

6.
hat
costume
curtain
mask
→ _____

Relativpronomen

4 Meine Theatergruppe. Übersetze die Sätze.

Wir treffen uns alle zweimal in der Woche.

_____

Jane hat sich selbst beigebracht, wie man ein Theaterstück aufführt.

_____

Peter macht viele Requisiten selbst.

_____

Nach einem Theaterstück schauen wir uns immer auf Video an.

_____ on video after a play.

Ich kann mich vor einem Theaterstück nie entspannen.

_____

Bedingungssätze

5 Ein Vorsprechen. Ergänze die richtige Form der Verben.

If I hadn't been to the theatre, I _____ (not/find out) that I like plays. If I _____ (not/like) plays, I wouldn't want to be an actor. I wouldn't have known about the audition if I _____ (not/see) the poster. If I don't go to the audition, I _____ (not/know) if I'm good enough – but I'm so scared. My friends ask me why I'm scared. "If you _____ (not/be) good enough, you won't get the part. That's no problem. If you practise more and learn more, you _____ (get) a part some time." If I wasn't so shy, it probably _____ (not/be) a problem. "If most famous actors hadn't done many auditions, they _____ (never/become) famous," say my friends. I don't think I want to be famous. "Why don't you just be a director?" asked my mum. Oh yes, what a good idea!

Die Zukunft

6 Nächste Woche. Unterstreiche die richtigen Formen der Verben.

I'm going/'ll have gone to Liverpool on Monday. My plane arrives/will have arrived at four and I'm going to stay/will have stayed with a family for two weeks. I'm meeting/'ll have met the family by Monday evening. I hope we'll like/'ll have liked each other. I hope by the end of my holiday I'm going to improve/'ll have improved my English a lot. Well, I'm sure it'll be/'ll have been better than now.

Übersetzung

7 Einkaufen. Übersetze diese Sätze.

Deine Hose sieht gut aus. Hast du sie selbst gemacht? Wie viele Hosen hast du jetzt?

_____

_____

Finde die Fehler

8 Besuch auf einem Bauernhof. Lies den Text und korrigiere die Fehler.

Last summer I stayed on ~~farm~~ and it was great.   → a farm;

~~The~~ life is very different on a farm and it seemed   → Life

strangely at first but I soon got used to it. The parents   _____

worked hardly every day and they didn't have much   _____

time to relax themselves, but life was slower on the   _____

farm. Nobody seemed to be in hurry. The mother   _____

usually cooked the lunch and we all ate it together.   _____

The food always smelt deliciously and everybody   _____

was always hungry after a day outside in the fields.   _____

I liked life of the farmer so much that I want to be   _____

farmer now. It would be easier if my parents are   _____

farmers, too, but I'll learn even if I have to teach   _____

everything.   _____

Zuhören und Notizen machen 🔊 18

9 Höre dir das Telefongespräch an. Notiere, was die Anruferin Ellis mitteilt: den Namen, die Telefonnummer im Büro und den Grund des Anrufs.

_____

_____

_____

Sprechen: Jemandem helfen/sich entschuldigen

10 Du bist mit deinem Vater in London. Er möchte einer älteren Frau helfen, aber sein Englisch reicht nicht aus. Vermittle zwischen den beiden.

Vater: Die Frau dort hat eine schwere Tasche. Frag sie, ob wir ihr helfen können.

Du: _____

Frau: Oh, yes please. That's very kind of you. I'm sorry I can't walk so quickly.

Du: _____

_____

Vater: Sag ihr, sie soll sich Zeit lassen.

Du: _____

(Dein Vater lässt eine Tasche fallen, und etwas geht kaputt.)

Vater: Oh! Sag ihr, dass es mir furchtbar leid tut!

Du: _____

Frau: Don't worry about it. It's no problem.

Du: _____

Zuhören, lesen und schreiben 🔊 19

11 Höre dir den Dialog an: Ein Mädchen spricht mit ihrem Bruder. Dann lies die zwei Briefe an die *agony aunt* durch. Wie heißt das Mädchen, das im Dialog spricht?

> Dear Linda,
>
> I love my best friend's boyfriend. He's been in our class since we started school and I've always liked him. We both liked him. He asked her to go out with him at Christmas and I've tried not to be jealous. And I'm still friends with both of them. Anyway last week he told me that he likes me more than my friend and he wants to go out with me now. What should I do? I really want to go out with him but I don't want to lose my friend.
>
> Sophie

> Dear Linda,
>
> My best friend's boyfriend kissed me last Saturday and I don't know if I should tell her or not. I like her boyfriend but I would never go out with him. I didn't want to kiss him (although he is nice and very good-looking!). If I tell her, she'll probably be angry with me and I don't think I've done anything wrong. But I also think I should tell her because it's not right that her boyfriend kisses other girls. Please tell me what I should do.
>
> Louise

→ Das Mädchen heißt _____.

12 Beantworte die Fragen über Sophie und Louise mit *true* oder *false*.

1. Sophie kissed her best friend's boyfriend, Paul. _____

2. Paul asked Sophie to go out with him at the youth club. _____

3. Louise's best friend is angry with her. _____

4. Louise would like to go out with her best friend's boyfriend. _____

13 Lies die Antwort der *agony aunt* zu dem Brief in Übung 11. Zu welchem Brief passt sie?

Dear …,
It's a very difficult situation and only you can decide. Who's more important to you: your friend or her boyfriend? And remember that you're young and you'll probably know your friend when you're both twenty and you probably won't know her boyfriend. If you cannot decide or you aren't sure, you should say "no". If he doesn't like your friend enough, they'll split up anyway and if he likes you enough and you like him enough, you can both wait and maybe it won't be such a problem later.

→ Die Antwort passt zum Brief von _____.

Versuche beim Schreiben immer, die Sätze einfach zu halten, dann sind sie verständlicher und weniger fehleranfällig.

14 Jetzt bist du die *agony aunt*. Nimm die Notizen zu Hilfe und verwende eigene Ideen, um den Brief von Louise aus Übung 11 zu beantworten.

| if – tell – friend/friend – angry | if – I – you/watch – boyfriend |

| probably – they – split up – anyway | if – see him – with other girls/tell – friend |

_____
_____
_____
_____

Unit 5

Wortschatz 5

Medien

1 Löse das Kreuzworträtsel und stelle aus den farbig hinterlegten Buchstaben das Lösungswort zusammen.

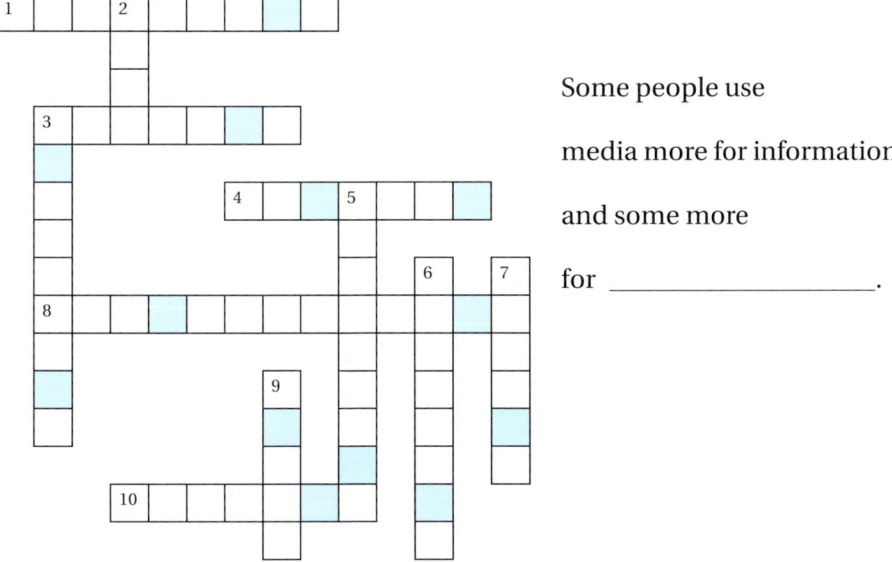

Some people use media more for information and some more for _____.

across:
1. I always read a … in the morning.
3. A … newspaper is one which many people read.
4. I'm going to a … tonight to hear my favourite band.
8. The director is making an … now. It's for a type of soap.
10. There's more news in a … newspaper.

down:
2. I watch a … every Tuesday and Thursday. It's about a few families.
3. Which is your favourite TV …?
5. I met a … last night but I've forgotten his name already.
6. That article has a great …
7. They make TV programmes in a …
9. TV and the Internet are both …

5 | Wortschatz | Grammatik | Leseverstehen | Hörverstehen

Beim Casting

2 Finde acht Verben in der Buchstabenschlange. Mit welchen Substantiven verwendet man sie normalerweise?

rewrite discover cast advertise reread design film photograph

_____	**an actor**	_____	**a script**
_____		_____	**a contract**
_____	**an ad**	_____	**a product**

Tipp: Lerne neue Verben immer im Zusammenhang mit Substantiven oder ganzen Sätzen, dann weißt du gleich, wie man sie verwendet. Überlege: Mit welchen Substantiven kannst du die Verben aus Übung 2 noch verwenden?

3 Löse die Anagramme auf und trage die Wörter in die richtigen Lücken ein.

tarconct – diess – sistastan – tingasc – tripsc – lenvoice – kolo – genta

My _____, John, contacted me last night about a _____. He sent me the _____ for the film but I didn't really like it. There was too much _____ for my taste. But it's difficult to get work and John thinks I have the right _____. The director's _____ is going to send me the _____ tomorrow and I'll learn them before the casting. Then if I'm lucky, I'll have the _____ in my pocket in a couple of weeks.

96

Wortschatz 5

Verben

4 Übersetze die farbig markierten Verben.

I'd like to create something beautiful. _____

I don't copy anybody's look. _____

She's become an actress and she's changed. _____

Let's exchange telephone numbers. _____

Ein Unfall

5 Lies den folgenden Text und vervollständige die fehlenden Wörter.

Yesterday I was just walking p_____ the cinema when somebody on the roof got my a_____. I saw that it was a boy who was wearing red and blue and just then, he fell o_____ . Or did he? I found out that he had jumped off because he thought he was Superman. Anyway he c_____ his leg on some glass on the floor and he also had a big g_____ in his arm. It was bleeding terribly and so I called an a_____. While we were waiting for the ambulance, I t_____ a bandage around the gashes on his arm and leg. I had my sports clothes in my bag and so I used those as b_____. The boy was very scared because there was b_____ everywhere and so I tried to d_____ him. First I told him jokes and then I made him paper planes with some paper out of my bag. I had r_____ him but there was a problem. I used my homework to make the planes. I'm very sorry, Mr Ellis, but that's why I haven't got my homework with me!

97

5 | Wortschatz | Grammatik | Leseverstehen | Hörverstehen

Menschen

6 Finde in dem Buchstabengitter neun Wörter, die Personen bezeichnen. Gib an, ob sie für Männer (m), Frauen (w) oder für beide Geschlechter (m/w) gelten.

_____

_____

_____

_____

_____

_____

_____

_____

_____

e	w	c	e	l	e	b	r	i	t	y
h	b	y	z	l	c	a	o	u	p	c
e	o	o	f	u	j	k	v	x	a	b
c	o	u	c	h	p	o	t	a	t	o
t	k	t	g	e	v	i	z	t	i	g
q	w	h	f	s	b	c	h	k	e	u
h	o	u	s	e	w	i	f	e	n	y
a	r	d	b	a	g	e	n	t	t	k
y	m	a	s	s	i	s	t	a	n	t

Adjektive

7 Übersetze diese Adjektive.

violent _____   realistic _____

basic _____   super _____

awesome _____   smooth _____

main _____   tight _____

Wiederholung: Das Perfekt und die einfache Form der Vergangenheit

Du verwendest das **present perfect,** wenn eine Handlung etwas mit dem *present* (Gegenwart) zu tun hat, wenn also die Auswirkung noch spürbar ist.

I**'ve broken** my arm. I broke it yesterday and it's still broken now.
She**'s eaten** too much. She feels terrible now.
I**'ve been** to Africa. I know what it's like.

Du verwendest das **present perfect** auch, wenn du sagen willst, dass etwas neulich passiert ist, du aber keinen Zeitpunkt nennst.

He**'s written** a new book. (Wann ist nicht wichtig.)

Du verwendest das **simple past,** wenn du sagen möchtest, wann etwas passiert ist.

I **broke** my arm **yesterday.**
She **ate** too much **for lunch.**

Wenn du über einen bestimmten Fall redet, der in der Vergangenheit passiert ist, verwendest du ebenfalls das **present perfect,** auch wenn du nicht ausdrücklich angibst, wann er passiert ist.

There **has been** a plane crash. *Aber:* The plane **had** problems when it was landing.

Signalwörter für das *present perfect*: never, ever, so far, already, yet, just; für das *simple past*: yesterday, in 2003, ... ago, when

8 Nach einem Casting. Unterstreiche die richtigen Verbformen.

Sue: Has the casting gone/Did the casting go well on Saturday?

Rob: No, it hasn't/didn't. I have been/was really nervous. I've tried/tried to forget it but I can't because it has been/was so embarrassing.

Sue: Maybe you have been/were better than you have thought/thought. Have you heard/Did you hear from the director?

Rob: No, I haven't/didn't, but I just phoned/'ve just phoned him and his assistant has said/said we may hear tomorrow.

Das Passiv

> Wenn du die Handlung betonen willst und nicht, wer für die Handlung verantwortlich ist, verwendest du Passivsätze.
>
> **Aktiv:** The assistant called my name.
>
> **Passiv:** My name was called.
>
> Im Passivsatz ist *my name* das Subjekt. Es ist nicht wichtig, wer gerufen hat. Im Aktivsatz ist das Subjekt *the assistant*.
>
> Die passiven Verbformen setzen sich aus einer Form von **to be** und dem **past participle** zusammen.
>
> | | |
> |---|---|
> | simple present | This programme **is made** in our town. Actors often **aren't paid** well. |
> | simple past | **Was** this TV programme **made** in England? We **were chosen** for the play. |
> | present perfect | **Have** you ever **been filmed**? These books **haven't been sold** yet. |

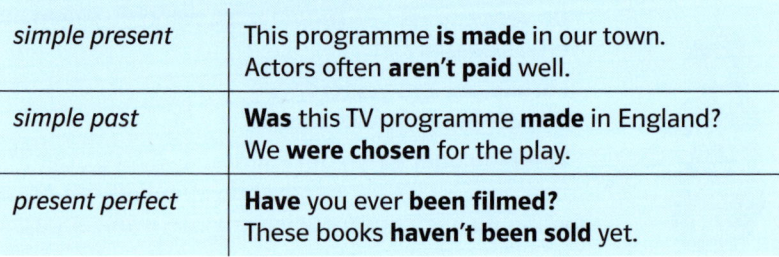

9 Sieh dir die Sätze an. Sind sie aktiv oder passiv? Unterstreiche jeweils das Subjekt des Satzes.

Media has become more important in the last twenty years or so. _____

The first newspapers were made thousands of years ago. _____

How much is the radio listened to in your house? _____

Many people still read books every day. _____

TV was first watched in the 1920's. _____

Has the Internet ever been used by more people? _____

Have newspapers ever been all true? _____

 Manche Verben können nicht ins Passiv gesetzt werden, z.B. Verben, die kein Akkusativobjekt bei sich haben, wie z. B. *go, come, be, become*.

Grammatik 5

10 Bilde aus den Satzteilen Passivsätze im *simple present*.

many films – make – in America

_____

the radio – listen to – everywhere

_____

books – not – read – as much now

_____

the Internet – use for – almost everything

_____

films – often – watch – in the cinema – ?

_____

11 Ergänze die angegebenen Verben in der richtigen Formen des Passivs.

Televisions _____ (first/make) not long before 1930 and _____ (sell) about ten years later. Televisions have changed a lot but they _____ (still/use) to watch films, news and programmes. The pictures on the televisions _____ (improve) a lot and now, of course, the films _____ (listen) to, too. We still watch them in our living room, but now the channel _____ (usually/change) from the sofa. It _____ (once/think) that if everybody had a TV, nobody would listen to the radio. That hasn't happened. The radio _____ (still/listened) to.

101

Vom Aktiv ins Passiv

> Wenn du einen Aktivsatz in einen Passivsatz umwandeln willst, musst du das Objekt des Aktivsatzes als Subjekt des Passivsatzes verwenden und das Subjekt entsprechend der Verbform ändern.
>
> Two boys have stolen my book. → **My book has been stolen.**
>
> Wenn es von Bedeutung ist, wer die Aktion ausführt, verwendest du den *by-agent*.
>
> | | subject | | object |
> |---|---|---|---|
> | *active* | My dad | made | that film. |
> | *passive* | **That film** | **was made** | **by my dad.** |
> | | subject | | by-agent |

12 Formuliere die Sätze im Passiv, wenn notwendig, mit *by-agent*.

J. K. Rowling finished the first Harry Potter book in 1995.

_____

People have translated the books into 65 languages.

_____

Children and older people read the books.

_____

People have made the books into films.

_____

They filmed the scenes in many different places.

_____

Daniel Radcliffe plays Harry Potter.

_____

Grammatik 5

Weitere Zeitformen des Passivs

> **Past perfect passive:** had been + past participle
>
> Du verwendest das *past perfect*, um zu sagen, was vor anderen Handlungen in der Vergangenheit passiert ist. Es wird oft verwendet mit *already, after, when, as soon as*.
>
> The script **had been** written before the actors were chosen. – Das Drehbuch war geschrieben worden, bevor die Schauspieler ausgesucht wurden.
> The book **had already sold** many copies before it was even written. – Das Buch war schon mehrfach verkauft worden, bevor es überhaupt geschrieben war.
>
> **Will future passive:** will be + past participle
>
> Das *will future* verwendest du, um Vermutungen über die Zukunft auszudrücken oder zu sagen, was passieren wird, ohne dass du darauf Einfluss nehmen kannst.
>
> I'm sure the film **will be watched** by millions. – Ich bin sicher, der Film wird Millionen Zuschauer haben.

13 Baue Passivsätze mit dem *will future* oder dem *past perfect*.

Liz – already – to offer – lots of parts – by her sixteenth birthday

_____ by her sixteenth birthday

she – hope – she – to give – many more roles

She hopes _____

I – never – to photograph – before my casting

_____

I – to photograph – a lot – in the future

_____

we – think – we – to interview – a lot – now that we are stars

_____

14 Bücher! Trage die Verben in der richtigen Passivform ein.

The future of books _____ (often/worry) about by many people. They think that fewer books _____ (make) in the future because people will watch more and more TV or because information, for example, _____ (download) onto the mobile or the computer when it _____ _____ (need). But is this realistic? Books _____ _____ (always/read). Well, almost! Books _____ (write) before modern paper _____ (first/make). Of course, they _____ (not/buy) by many people because they were too expensive. In the time of the Romans books _____ (even/borrow) from libraries. People were once worried about the future of the radio but history has shown us that the more different media _____ (use), the more important they become.

15 Aktiv oder Passiv? Formuliere ganze Sätze.

the Internet – first – to use – by the public – in the 1990s

_____

scientists – to use – the Internet – before then

_____

a web browser – to need – when you want to use the Internet

_____ when you want to use the Internet.

Das Passiv bei Verben mit zwei Objekten

> Viele Verben werden mit zwei Objekten gebraucht, z.B. **give, offer, send, sell, show.**
> The director has offered **the actor a role.**
> → *The actor* und *a role* sind beides Objekte.
> In einem Passivsatz können beide Objekte zum Subjekt gemacht werden.
> **The actor** has been offered a role → **passive 1/personal passive**
> **A role** has been offered to the actor → **passive 2**
> Wenn die Person Subjekt des Satzes wird, spricht man vom persönlichen Passiv. Diese Möglichkeit gibt es im Deutschen nicht! Wenn du das *personal passive* übersetzen willst, benutze „man".
> I was asked a question. – Man stellte mir eine Frage.
> Das *personal passive* ist im Englischen gebräuchlicher als das *passive 2*. Dieses verwendet man oft, wenn dieses Objekt sehr lang ist oder es betont werden soll. Wenn die Person am Ende des Satzes kommt, wird es mit *to* angehängt.
> The invitation was given **to our whole family.**

16 John geht zu einem Casting. Gib die angegebenen Aktivsätze mit beiden Formen des Passivs wieder. Welches ist das *personal passive*?

The agent sent John his sides.

_____

_____

At the casting the assistant gave John a number.

_____

_____

The director offered John his first big role.

_____

_____

17 Im Fernsehstudio. Stehen die Sätze im Aktiv oder im Passiv? Trage „active", „passive" oder, wo das *personal passive* verwendet wird, „pp" ein.

1. Yesterday I was given a ticket for the television studios. _____

2. I've wanted to go there for years. _____

3. We had a great time. _____

4. We were shown all the studios and the actors rooms. _____

5. We were even filmed on a stage. _____

6. I hope I'll be offered a part in their next soap. _____

18 Reich und berühmt? Schreibe diesen Text neu, indem du das Passiv verwendest. Benutze das *personal passive,* wo möglich.

Somebody invited me to my first celebrity party last night. First they showed us the host's new film and then they gave us lots of food and drink. Some famous French cooks made the food and it tasted delicious. A band played some great music and people told us lots of funny stories. People made lots of new friends but nobody even asked me what my name was.

_____

_____

_____

_____

_____

_____

Tipp Bevor du einen Aktivsatz in einen Passivsatz umwandelst, unterstreiche die Objekte!

Lesen und schreiben: Zeitungsberichte

Zeitungsberichte haben normalerweise folgende Struktur:	
headline (Überschrift)	Wovon handelt der Artikel?
erster Absatz	die wichtigsten Informationen: Wo?, Wann?, Wer?, Was?
folgende Abschnitte	weitere Einzelheiten und Hintergrundinformationen
Schluss	weitere nützliche Informationen – je nachdem, wie viel Platz zur Verfügung steht

Das Passiv wird in Zeitungsartikeln oft verwendet. Es klingt formeller und ist nützlich, wenn man nicht genau weiß, wer was getan hat.

19 Lies die Zeitungsartikel und wähle jeweils die beste Überschrift, indem du ihr einen Buchstaben zuordnest.

A.
Alan Wisdom has been hurt at the TV studios in Manchester. They were filming the soap *Coronation Street* when a fire started in the studios. Alan Wisdom and two cameramen were taken to hospital but are not badly hurt. It is not known how the fire started.
It is thought that the fire started at about 2 pm in one of the studios. The police and fire experts are examining the area. A man was seen in the area at lunchtime and the police are trying to find out who the man was. Wisdom and the cameramen were hurt when they were walking past the studio and a window broke. Wisdom was cut by glass on his face and neck.
Alan Wisdom has been with the soap for two years and plays one of the more popular characters. It is not known when he will be able to film again or if the writers will write his bandages into the script. Most people think that the fire was started by the man who was seen in the studio. "We don't know who the man was or why he was there. Maybe it was an angry actor who wasn't cast in a TV programme," said one man at the studios.

B.
Fifty-five people were hurt after violence at the Manchester United football ground, Old Trafford, last night. All fifty-five were taken to hospital and most were allowed to go home again later. Six fans were badly hurt and are still in hospital.

The United against Liverpool game started quietly but after twenty-five minutes the violence started at the United end. Bottles were thrown and one player, Mark Scholes, was hit on the head and had to go to hospital. A fight started and fans ran on to the pitch. The Police stopped the violence after about twenty minutes and the game started again.

Fans at the game said that it was not United fans who started the violence. Some said that some Liverpool fans were sitting at the United end and others said that it wasn't football fans who started the violence. One man said, "There was a crowd of men near me who were not interested in the game. I saw that they had bottles with them. I don't know how they brought them into the stadium." United won the game two – nil. It is not yet known when Mark Scholes will be able to play again.

C.
Yesterday evening a boy was badly hurt on his way home from school. It is thought that Mark Royle was attacked by three youths as he turned into Church Street but the police have not been able to question him yet. He is in hospital and is still too shocked to be able to talk about what happened. It happened at four thirty in the Church Street area of town. James Roberts was walking down the street when he saw Mark Royle on the floor. He didn't see what happened but he saw two youths who were running around the corner. Roberts called the police and the ambulance and Royle was taken to hospital right away. Mark Royle had been to drama club and was walking home when he was attacked. It is not known why he was attacked. The youths didn't steal anything. The police would like to ask anybody who saw anything to phone Northampton police on 01232 543 654.

mögliche Überschriften:

Player Hurt at Old Trafford _____   Fire in *Coronation Street* _____

Boy Attacked Three Youths _____   Violence at Football Match _____

Alan Wisdom Hurt in Fire _____   Boy Attacked after School _____

20 Unterstreiche die grundsätzlichen Informationen in jedem Text doppelt, also: wo, wann, wer, was? Unterstreiche weitere wichtige Information einfach. Dann beantworte die folgende Fragen.

1. Who was taken to hospital after the fire? _____

2. Where did the fire happen? _____

3. When did the fire start? _____

4. How were the men hurt? _____

5. What happened at Old Trafford? _____

6. How was Mark Scholes hurt? _____

7. How many fans are still in hospital? _____

8. What happened to Mark Royle? _____

9. When and where did it happen? _____

10. Who should phone 01232 543 654? _____

21 Ein Museumsraub. Lies die Aussage eines Zeugen und die Polizeimeldung, dann verfasse einen Zeitungsartikel, in dem du die Informationen zusammenfasst.

> I was walking behind the Tate Gallery last night at about 8 pm and I saw two men. They were climbing out of a window. And they were carrying something. Maybe they stole that famous painting. They were wearing masks and their clothes were black.

```
Monet painting
stolen.

8 pm last night.
Anybody with infor-
mation should phone
0208 566 2131.
```

_____
_____
_____
_____
_____
_____

Versuche deine Sätze einfach zu halten. Du brauchst dir hier keine Synonyme einfallen lassen: Verwende die Begriffe aus vorgegebenen Texten.

Zuhören: *Strong and weak sounds* 🎧 20

22 Höre dir die vier Kurzdialoge an und spreche sie nach. Sieh dir die farbig markierten Wörter an und unterstreiche diejenigen, die in ihrer starken Form gesprochen sind.

1. Who's that present for?

   It's for Ann.

2. Where do you want to go to?

   I'd like to go to London.

3. Can you help me with this, please?

   Yes, I can.

4. Was the play good?

   Yes, it was. It was excellent.

Zuhören: *Media in your life* 🎧 21

23 Höre dir die Stellungnahmen der drei Jugendlichen an. Welches Bild passt am besten zu wem? Warum sind Medien für die drei wichtig?

music maniac **couch potato** **bookworm** **super surfer**

_____   _____   _____   _____

Media is important for …

Linda to _____

Jake _____

Jake _____

Zuhören: Vorschläge machen 🎧 22

24 Ann übt eine Rolle für ein Casting. Ihr Freund Mark berät sie. Welche der Sätze werden von Ann gesagt, welche von Mark? Achtung Falle: Manche kommen im Dialog gar nicht vor!

Well, I think you should …   _____

Yes, that's a good idea.   _____

What did you think?   _____

That's rubbish.   _____

I'll do that.   _____

I'll think about it.   _____

And I think it would be better if …   _____

If you think you're better, why don't you …   _____

And if I were you, I'd …   _____

Tipp → Bevor du einen Hörtext anhörst, sieh dir immer zuerst die Fragen an, die sich auf den Text beziehen. So kannst du schon Informationen herausfinden, bevor du zuhörst.

25 Unterstreiche die Aussagen, die richtig sind.

Mark thinks that Ann will/won't get the part.

He thinks that Ann should speak more slowly/loudly/angrily.

He thinks that Ann should move her arms/head/legs/mouth.

Ann has to say the words: "I love you." / "I have you." / "I hate you".

Mark thinks that Ann should change everything/was excellent.

| 6 | Wortschatz | Grammatik | Leseverstehen | Hörverstehen |

Unit 6

Auf Reisen

1 Beschrifte die Bilder.

1. _____ 2. _____ 3. _____

4. _____ 5. _____ 6. _____

2 Welche Wörter sind hier umschrieben? Stelle aus den hinterlegten Buchstaben das Lösungswort zusammen.

1. It's like a trip but usually longer. → _ _ _ _ _ _ _

2. A country must have one of these if you want to go by train. → _ _ _ _ _ _ _ _

3. A kind of pasta from China. → _ _ _ _ _ _

4. When you arrive at a friendly place, you get a warm one. → _ _ _ _ _ _ _

5. In many countries English is this. → _ _ _ _ _   _ _ _ _ _ _ _ _

6. Journeys can take longer because of one of these. → _ _ _ _ _

7. An area with lots of grass in America. → _ _ _ _ _ _ _

Lösungswort: Today travelling isn't usually _____.

Menschen

3 Finde die acht Personenbezeichnungen und ordne sie richtig zu.

burglarfirefightermankindparamedicprincesspoliceofficertravellermissionary

the world _____

foreign countries _____

foreign churches _____

castle _____

hospital _____

police station _____

people's houses _____

fire station _____

To take

4 Übersetze *to take* jeweils dem Zusammenhang gemäß.

1. My journey by bike to Spain took two weeks. _____

2. Can you take that away from me? It's horrible. _____

3. I'm going to take my aunt a nice present when I visit her. _____

4. Somebody's taken my bag. _____

Vergiss nicht den Unterschied zwischen *bring* und *take*: Bring bewegt immer etwas in Richtung auf den Sprecher hin *(Bring that here, please)*, take bedeutet immer eine Bewegung vom Sprecher anderswohin *(I'm going to take it with me)*.

Verben

5 Ersetze jeweils das farbig markierte Verb durch ein anderes.

1. She rescued me. She _____
2. He's finished the project. He's _____
3. He went more slowly later. He _____
4. We became less and less interested. We _____
5. I'd suggest you read this book. I'd _____

Adjektive: Situationen beschreiben

6 Löse die Buchstabenrätsel auf, um Adjektive zu finden, die die genannten Situationen am besten beschreiben.

sadipingtinpo – soudearng – flauw –yonannig – sticfanta – engrigfhtin

1. They were walking on the prairie when the buffalo passed them. They were lucky. If they had been in the buffalo's path, they would not have survived.

→ _____

2. We went to Spain and we loved every minute. We met very nice people and saw lots of wild animals. I want to go again.

→ _____

3. We really wanted to climb to the top of the mountain. We had trained for months and taken all the right clothes and then the weather was too bad and we couldn't climb it.

→ _____

4. I went swimming in the sea near California and suddenly I saw a shark. I didn't know what to do at all. I stayed there and it swam away. Later I found out that they don't attack people.

→ _____

5. I just wanted to sleep on the plane but this guy talked all the time. At first I was polite but then I just listened to my mp3 player … and he still didn't stop.

→ _____

6. The place was noisy. Everything was too expensive. There wasn't much to do there. And even the weather was bad for the time of year.

→ _____

Verben für *to say*

7 Finde in dem Buchstabengitter sechs Verben, die man anstelle von *to say* verwenden kann, und trage sie im *simple past* dort ein, wo sie passen.

1. They _____ us to find a guide.

2. She _____, "Help, help!"

3. I _____ him not to swim alone.

4. She later _____ everything that was said at the meeting.

5. Julie _____ yesterday that you were going to France on holiday.

6. My dad _____ to give me some money.

A	D	V	I	S	E	P
W	G	K	V	A	R	Z
M	E	N	T	I	O	N
R	S	C	R	E	A	M
E	T	A	S	X	M	H
P	R	O	M	I	S	E
O	E	F	D	O	U	E
R	G	D	W	A	R	N
T	H	P	Y	C	I	Z

Verben und Substantive in der gleichen Form

8 Schreibe die Sätze um, indem du das farbig markierte Substantiv als Verb verwendest.

I did a lot of work last summer.

_____

We didn't have a fight all holiday.

_____

The taste of that plant is weird.

_____

There wasn't a lot of rain in Scotland last summer.

_____

Direkte und indirekte Rede

> *Direct speech:* John said, "I had a great holiday."
>
> *Indirect speech:* John said that he had had a great holiday.
>
> Die direkte Rede steht immer in Anführungszeichen. Nach dem einleitenden Verb der direkten Rede kommt ein Komma, und der Punkt am Satzende steht wie im Deutschen innerhalb der Anführungszeichen. Steht jedoch die direkte Rede zuerst, kommt ein Komma *vor* dem Anführungszeichen: "I had a great holiday," said John. Im Deutschen ist es andersherum: „Mein Urlaub war toll", sagte John.
>
> Die indirekte Rede besteht immer aus einem **Einleitungssatz** *(John said)* und einem **Folgesatz** *(that he had had a great holiday).*
>
> Zwischen dem Einleitungssatz und dem Folgesatz steht *kein* Komma – anders als im Deutschen!
>
> Das einleitende *that* kann auch weggelassen werden.

9 Schau dir die Sätze an und schreibe sie neu, indem du die nötigen Satzzeichen ergänzt.

1. My friend asked would you like to come to France with me. (direkte Rede)

2. She always says that France is a fantastic country. (indirekte Rede)

3. I'd really like to go to France I told my mum. (direkte Rede)

4. She said that I could go. (indirekte Rede)

Grammatik 6

Indirekte Rede mit Zeitverschiebung

Wenn das einleitende Verb in der Vergangenheit steht (z. B. *said*, *told*), findet im Folgesatz der indirekten Rede eine Verschiebung der Zeiten statt.

simple present → *simple past*	"I **like** France." → She said **she liked** France.
present progressive → *past progressive*	"I**'m travelling** around Spain." → She said she **was travelling** around Spain.
present perfect → *past perfect*	"I**'ve made** lots of friends." → He said he **had made** lots of friends.
simple past → *past perfect*	"I **had** a great time in Italy." → She said she **had had** a great time in Italy.
past perfect → *past perfect*	"I**'d** already **spent** my money." → He said he **had** already **spent** her money.
will → *would*	"I**'ll see** you next week." → She said she**'d see** us the following week.
can → *could*	"I **can** stay with friends." → She said she **could** stay with friends.

Auch die Pronomen müssen entsprechend geändert werden, z. B. *I* → *he*; *you* → *us*.

10 Kate ist in die USA gefahren. Schau dir die Sprechblasen an, dann unterstreiche die richtigen Verbformen in der indirekten Rede.

I'm having a great time.
I love it here.
I've been to lots of places.
I'll phone again tomorrow.

Kate phoned last night and she said she had had / was having a great time. She said she loved / has loved it there and that she went / 'd been to lots of places. And she said she'd phone / will phone again tomorrow.

117

11 Ein Unfall auf der Autobahn (M6). Ergänze die Sätze.

"There's been an accident on the M6."

The police reported that there _____.

"Two lorries crashed into each other."

They said that _____.

"One of the drivers had fallen asleep."

They explained that _____.

"We're moving the lorries now."

They said _____ then.

"We hope the road will be open in two hours."

They added that _____.

Zuhören und Wiedergeben 🎧 23

12 Höre dir an, was Kim ihrer Freundin am Telefon sagt, dann überlege, wie du ihre Aussagen in der indirekten Rede formulieren musst.

1. She said she was sitting/sat/had sat in a train.

2. She told me that she's left/she left/she'd just left Madrid.

3. But she said she didn't sleep/hasn't slept/hadn't slept there.

4. She added that they can sleep/could sleep/would sleep in the train.

5. She said she's already spent/already spent/had already spent all her money.

6. She told me she'll be/ she's/she'd be home tomorrow.

Zeitangaben in der indirekten Rede

> Zeitangaben werden beibehalten, wenn sie auch zum Zeitpunkt des Berichtens noch stimmen.
>
> "I'm playing football **this** evening." → Wenn diese Tatsache noch am gleichen Tag berichtet wird, also vor dem Abend, heißt es: She said she was playing football **this** evening.
>
> Wenn jedoch erst berichtet wird, wenn das Ereignis schon vorbei ist, heißt es: She said she was playing football **that** evening.
>
> Andere Zeitangaben ändern sich so:
>
> | | | | |
> |---|---|---|---|
> | today | → that day | three days ago | → three days before/earlier |
> | tonight | → that night | last week | → the week before/earlier |
> | this morning | → that morning | | |
> | tomorrow | → the next day/ the following day | yesterday | → the day before |
> | next year | → the next year/ the following year | | |
>
> Auch andere Wörter müssen geändert werden, um die verschiedenen Standpunkte zu verdeutlichen:
>
> "I like it **here**." → She said she liked it **there**.
>
> this → that; here → there
>
> come → go; bring → take

13 Menschen am Flughafen. Gib wieder, was diese Leute sagten.

"I bought my ticket for this flight yesterday."

He said _____

"We're flying tomorrow but we want to check in today."

She said _____

"I often come here because I like planes."

He said _____

| 14 | Lucy, in den Ferien bei ihrer Tante in Kalifornien, hinterlässt eine Nachricht auf dem Anrufbeantworter ihrer Mutter. Gib wieder, was sie gesagt hat. |

Hi. I'm having a great time here. Yesterday we went to Los Angeles and last night we watched a play. It was great. Tomorrow my cousin is coming here and she's bringing her new boyfriend with her. I'll tell you if he's nice. Next week we're going to the beach. I hope I can surf there. Anyway I'll phone you again.

Lucy said _____

_____

_____

_____

_____

_____

_____

_____

_____

_____

 Wenn du eine Unterhaltung berichtest, musst du nicht jedes einzelne Wort berichten – das Wichtigste genügt!

Zuhören und das Wichtigste berichten 🎧 24

| 15 | Höre dir an, was Rita auf den Anrufbeantworter spricht, und gib nur die drei wichtigsten Fakten wieder. |

She said _____

_____

_____

Die indirekte Rede mit Einführungssatz im Präsens

Wenn du gleich wiedergibst, was jemand gesagt oder geschrieben hat, verwendest du für das Einleitungsverb das *simple present*. Hier gibt es *keine* Zeitverschiebung.

"**I don't like my** new boat." → She says **she doesn't like her** new boat.

Andere Wörter ändern sich entsprechend der Situation, z. B. *my* → *her*.

16 Johns Oma hat angerufen. John erzählt seiner Mutter, was sie sagte. Manches erzählt er gleich und manches erst später. Was hat er seiner Mutter gleich erzählt?

1. She says she's going to Australia next week.
2. She said Grandad didn't want to go.
3. She says she's booked a holiday.
4. She told me that Aunt Ellen had invited her.

gleich: _____   später: _____

17 Chris' Vater ruft von unterwegs an. Chris spricht mit ihm und erzählt seiner Mutter anschließend, was sein Vater gesagt hat.

"I'll be late because there's been an accident."

He says _____

"I can't go on because the road has been closed."

_____

"You needn't make me any dinner."

_____

"You'll have to go to judo by bus."

_____

Fragen in der indirekten Rede

Fragen mit Fragewort: "**What did you do** yesterday?" → He asked me **what I had done** the day before.

"**Where do you** usually **go** on holiday?" → She wanted to know **where I** usually **went** on holiday.

"**When are you going** home?" → They wanted to know **when I was going** home.

Bei Fragen in der indirekten Rede werden die Hilfsverben *do*, *does* und *did* nicht verwendet. Die Satzstellung ist dieselbe wie in Aussagesätzen:

         Verb Subjekt   Subjekt Verb
          ↓   ↓   ↓   ↓

"Where **were you** yesterday?" → She asked me where **I had been** the day before.

Fragen ohne Fragewort: Wenn die Frage kein Fragewort beinhaltet, wird im Folgesatz *if* oder *whether* verwendet.

"**Do you like** it here?" → She asked me **if I liked** it there.

"**Have you ever been** here before?" → They wanted to know **whether we had ever been** here before.

18 Neil möchte mit Rob in die Ferien fahren. Neils Mutter hat einige Fragen dazu, von denen Neil später Rob berichtet. Setze in die indirekte Rede.

"Where do you want to go?"

She asked me _____

"How will you get there?"

She wanted to know _____

"Do you have enough money?"

_____

"Have Rob's parents agreed?"

_____

19 Zara wird Zeugin eines Unfalls und ruft den Notarzt. Später erzählt sie ihrer Mutter von dem Telefonat. Vervollständige die Lücken.

Zara: Hello. I've just seen an accident.
Woman: Where are you calling from?
Zara: I'm on the corner of Church Street and London Road.
Woman: OK. The police are on their way. Has anybody been hurt?
Zara: I don't know but I think somebody is trapped in their car.
Woman: OK. We'll send an ambulance and the fire service. Are you OK? What's your name?

I phoned 999 and I said that _____ an accident. The

woman asked me _____ and I said

that I _____ on the corner of Church Street and London Road.

She told me then that the police _____ on their way and asked

me _____. I said I _____

_____ but I _____ in the car.

She said that _____ an ambulance and the fire

service and asked me _____ and _____

_____. It was very exciting.

20 Dennis ist am Flughafen zufällig Amanda begegnet. Welche Fragen haben sie einander gestellt? Sieh dir die Sätze in der indirekten Rede an und rekonstruiere die direkte Rede.

He asked her where she was going to.

_____

She asked him if he liked flying.

_____

He wanted to know whether she had ever been to Australia before.

_____

Indirekte Aufforderungssätze

"Please **turn** all laptops off now." → They asked us **to turn** our laptops off.

"**Don't leave** your seats." → She told us **not to leave** our seats.

Aufforderungssätze werden als Infinitivkonstruktion mit **to** oder **not to** wiedergegeben.

Man kann sie mit den Verben **ask, tell, warn** und **remind** einleiten. **Warn** wird immer mit **not** verwendet.

"**Don't drive** too fast." → They warned us **not to drive** too fast. (Sie ermahnten uns, nicht zu schnell zu fahren.)

21 Als Neil mit Rob in die Ferien aufbricht, geben ihm seine Eltern gute Ratschläge. Wie erzählt er Rob, was sie zu ihm gesagt haben?

"Phone me when you arrive."

My mum told me _____ when I arrive.

"Be careful on your bike."

My dad advised me _____

"Don't get too tired."

My mum warned me _____

"Look after your bike well."

My mum told me _____

"Don't ask me for more money."

My dad told me _____

22 Neil ruft zu Hause an. Anschließend berichtet seine Mutter seinem Vater, was Neil ihr erzählt hat. Ergänze die Lücken.

Can you send me some more money, please?

Don't worry about us.

We've arrived in Cornwall.

We're having a great time.

I can't find my anorak. Is it at home?

He said they _____ a great time but he asked me _____

_____. He told me _____ and

said that _____ in Cornwall. He said that _____

_____ his anorak and asked _____ at home.

Zuhören und berichten 🎧 25

23 Ein paar Straßen weiter ist ein Feuer ausgebrochen. Höre dir den CD-Track an: Eine Polizistin gibt Sicherheitshinweise für die Anwohner durch. Gib wieder, was sie gesagt hat, indem du als Einleitungsverb *asked*, *said* oder *told* verwendest.

She said _____

_____

_____

_____

_____

Lesen: Ein Segelurlaub

24 Lies die Geschichte einmal durch, um das Wesentliche zu verstehen. Dann entscheide dich für die beste Zusammenfassung.

"I asked my mum if I could go on the sailing holiday," said Mary after she'd arrived at Julia's house.
"And what did she say?" asked Julia.
"Well, she said I could learn to sail here and wanted to know why I wanted
5 to go on a holiday for a week."
"And did you explain how exciting it would be to sleep in a boat on the sea?"
"Yes, I did. And I think she understood a bit but she still thinks I'm too young."
10 "So you can't come?"
"Yes, I can. My dad convinced her. Good old dad!" cried Mary happily.
"Oh, great," said Julia, "I'm so excited. Four weeks and we can go. I wonder if we'll meet some nice people there."
"I hope so. Do you think we'll be able to swim in the sea?" asked Mary, and
15 they talked about it all night.

It was the fifth of August and Julia and Mary had been sailing on the *Good Hope* for two days.
"How are you?" asked Julia.
"Oh, I still feel terrible," said Mary. "I can't believe it. I never thought that I
20 would feel sick. I've been on boats lots of times."
"Well, just relax. You'll feel better soon. The captain said it can take a few days before you get used to it."
Mary just stood on the boat and looked at the sea. She felt better like that. She hadn't sailed herself at all up to then. When she moved, she was sick.
25 But she watched the others and so she'd learnt things. She was still glad that she'd come because the weather was good and the people were nice. She'd even seen a whale one day.
On the sixth of August she woke up early and thought something felt different. What was it? Then she knew. She didn't feel sick any more. She
30 jumped up out of the very small bed and banged her head. "Ow," she cried, but it didn't stop her. She ran outside and joined the others for breakfast. They all cheered when they saw that she no longer felt sick. And the rest of the day was wonderful. They all worked together well as a team and Mary could help now, too. The wind became stronger and the boat flew over the
35 waves. It was a fantastic feeling. But it didn't last long.

The wind became stronger and stronger and they had to put the sails down so that they could control the boat. The sky went dark with black clouds and the waves became bigger and bigger. Mary started to feel sick again but even worse; she became scared, too.

40 "Put your life jackets *(Schwimmwesten)* on now," said the captain. "A storm is coming."

Everybody put their life jackets on and tied themselves to the boat so that they wouldn't be washed away by the waves. The captain had heard on the radio that a storm was coming but it had come more quickly than he had 45 expected. And it was worse than they had thought.

There was nothing they could do. They just had to wait. It got darker and darker – night was falling, and there was no sign that the storm was coming to an end. Nobody was laughing now. Then suddenly they heard a loud crash and the boat jumped. They had hit something. Somebody screamed.

50 Would the boat sink now? The captain used the radio and called for help quickly. He looked over the side of the boat. There was a hole in it but it was a small hole. They hoped that help would come before the boat sank.

They waited and waited. Would anybody be able to come out in this storm? Then they heard a helicopter and saw its lights. It came nearer and nearer 55 but then turned around and went back again. There was nothing it could do. A short time later they heard a lifeboat. They saw the lights. They got nearer and nearer but then they stopped.

"I don't think they can come nearer in this weather," said the captain, "the rocks are too dangerous."

60 Nobody said anything. The boat was filling with water. It was sinking.

"I wish I'd stayed at home," thought Mary.

mögliche Zusammenfassungen:
a) Mary and Julia go on holiday by boat. Before they arrive, there's a bad storm and Mary feels sick.
b) Mary and Julia stay on a boat on the sea on holiday. There's a terrible storm and Mary feels sick.
c) Mary and Julia learn to sail on holiday. Mary feels sick at first and later there's a bad storm.

Die beste Zusammenfassung ist _____ .

25 Lies die Fragen durch und wähle jeweils die richtige Antwort.

1. Why didn't Mary's mum want her to go on holiday? → _____
a) She thought it was dangerous.
b) She thought Mary was too young.
c) She thought it was too expensive.

2. How long did they want to stay on the boat? → _____
a) A week.
b) Four weeks.
c) Three days.

3. When did Mary feel better? → _____
a) On the second day.
b) On the third day.
c) On the fourth day.

4. When did the storm come? → _____
a) On the fifth of August.
b) On the sixth of August.
c) On the seventh of August.

5. What did they do when the wind got stronger? → _____
a) Called for help.
b) Went inside.
c) Tied themselves to the boat.

6. What came out in the storm? → _____
a) A helicopter.
b) A lifeboat.
c) A helicopter and a lifeboat.

26 Die Geschichte geht gut aus: Alle werden gerettet. Später erzählen sie, was an Bord geschah. Wo findest du die Informationen im Text? Gib die entsprechenden Zeilen an.

1. *Mary:* Julia told me that I'd feel better soon. _____

2. *Julia:* The captain told us all to put our life jackets on. _____

3. *Mary:* The boat hit a rock with a loud crash. _____

4. *Julia:* The captain didn't think the lifeboat could come nearer. _____

5. *Mary:* The boat started going down. _____

Zuhören: gleicher Klang, andere Schreibung 🔊 26

27 Höre dir die Sätze auf der CD an, dann kreuze jeweils die richtige Schreibweise der Wörter an, die gesprochen werden.

1. sea ☐   see ☐
2. whether ☐   weather ☐
3. right ☐   write ☐
4. brake ☐   break ☐
5. weak ☐   week ☐
6. road ☐   rode ☐

Zuhören: Ein Notfall 🔊 27

28 Höre dir die zwei Anrufe beim Notfalldienst an und beantworte dann die Fragen dazu.

Emergency 1

1. What's happened? _____
2. Where is the boy? _____
3. How many people have been hurt? _____
4. What are they going to send? _____

Emergency 2

1. What's happened? _____
2. Where is the girl? _____
3. How many people have been hurt? _____
4. What are they going to send? _____

Zuhören: Smalltalk 28

29 Höre dir erst den Dialog an, dann kreuze die richtigen Antworten an.

1. Where are they?
a) At the bus stop. ☐
b) In town. ☐
c) At a concert. ☐

2. What's the weather like?
a) Cold. ☐
b) Warm. ☐
c) Rainy. ☐

3. What month is it?
a) December. ☐
b) November. ☐
c) September. ☐

4. Which bus are they waiting for?
a) 24. ☐
b) 50. ☐
c) 15. ☐

5. What do they do at the end?
a) Wait for the bus. ☐
b) Take a taxi. ☐
c) Watch the band together. ☐

30 Höre dir CD-Track 28 ein zweites Mal an. Wie zeigen die Sprecher, dass sie einander zuhören und weitersprechen wollen? Vervollständige die Lücken.

Boy: Yeah, it's always late, _____?

Girl: _____. Last week I waited for half an hour.

Boy: And then two buses came together?

Girl: _____. But I hope it isn't too late today. _____.

Boy: _____, it's only September and it feels like December. (…) Yes, I'm going into town. _____?

Girl: _____, I'm going to town, too. I'm going to see 50 Cent.

Boy: _____? Oh, he's great, _____?

Revision C (Unit 5–6)

Menschen

1 Ordne die Bezeichnungen der richtigen Spalte zu.

athlete – empress – firefighter – knight – paramedic – princess – refereee – scientist – umpire

sport	royal	jobs

Odd one out

2 Sieh dir die Wortgruppen an. Ein Wort passt jeweils nicht hinein. Welches? Überlege: Zu welcher Kategorie gehören die anderen Wörter?

1. bellow
   scream → _____
   delay
   bang

2. bookworm
   spinach → _____
   cereal
   noodle

3. ad
   soap → _____
   programme
   channel

4. tour
   trip → _____
   traveller
   journey

Revision C — Rückblick / Ausblick

Kollokationen

3 Filmbusiness. Trage die fehlenden Verben in die Lücken ein.

I want to be an actress but I don't have awesome looks so I don't _____ attention everywhere I go. Next month a famous director is coming to our town and I'm going to _____ the chance to talk to him. He's trying to _____ money for a charity which he organises. He's going to discuss his ideas on the radio and _____ his opinion on the world's problems. I'm going to be in the studio, too, and I'm going to _____ him to give me a job. I'm going to _____ it.

Mixed bag

4 Eine Reise nach New York. Ergänze die passenden Wörter.

I'd always w_____ to go to New York because some cousins live there. Last summer I m_____ it there for the first time. I arrived there at the beginning of July and got a really warm w_____ from my cousins. They showed me a lot of the city and it is a_____, but then they had to go b_____ to work so I looked around on my own. They r_____ some museums and shops to visit and they also a_____ me which parts of town were safe. New York isn't so d_____ now but I still j_____ out of my skin when I heard a noise like a g_____. It wasn't, of course. Somebody had just opened a bottle of champagne.

132

Das Passiv

5 Aktiv oder Passiv? Setze die Verben richtig ein.

I _____ (already/give) small parts in plays in town when I saw the advertisement for a new TV soap. Actors _____ (need) from my town. I _____ (send) a letter and a photo right away and a few days ago I _____ (audition). It went well and I still can't believe it, but I _____ (offer) a part in the soap! It _____ (film) in our town and it _____ (see) by all my friends and family. I'm very excited. The only problem is that I'm playing a ghost and my face _____ (not/see) at all.

6 Schreibe die Sätze ins Passiv um. Verwende das *personal passive*, wo es möglich ist.

1. Last week they made a film in our town.

   _____

2. The director asked my friends lots of questions.

   _____

3. They gave me a little part in the film.

   _____

4. They will show the film to us in a few weeks.

   _____

Indirekte Rede

7 Bei einem Casting. Gib wieder, was der Regisseur gesagt hat.

"You will be called when it's your turn."

The director said _____

"Please act the scene in your sides now."

_____

"Have you ever acted before?"

_____

"Don't call us. We'll call you."

_____

8 Ryan trifft Kate zufällig am Bahnhof. Schau dir an, worüber sie sprechen, dann gib aus der Sicht von Ryan wieder, was sie gesagt haben.

I said that the train _____

Zuhören und sich Notizen machen 🎧 29

9 Höre dir das Telefongespräch zwischen Daniel und Judith an und unterstreiche die richtigen Aussagen.

1. Daniel is at the station / in the train / in Liverpool.

2. Daniel has been to Reading / Liverpool / Manchester.

3. Daniel had met some friends / some actors / some cousins there.

4. He went on a ferry to Ireland / to Manchester / across the Mersey.

5. Judith has heard about the casting / a party / Christmas.

6. She's got the ticket / the part / a present.

7. Daniel invites her to a party / to a play / to celebrate at his house.

8. Judith can't go / would love to go / doesn't want to go.

9. Judith invites Daniel to a party / to a play / to celebrate at her house.

10 Höre dir den Dialog auf CD-Track 29 noch einmal an, um deine Lösung zu überprüfen. Dann erzähle aus Daniels Sicht, indem du die Sätze aus Übung 9 in die indirekte Rede setzt.

Judith phoned and I told her I _____

Revision C — Rückblick | Ausblick

Mediation: Ein Unfall in England

11 Vermittle zwischen einer deutschen Zeugin und der Polizei.

Polizei: Can you tell me what you saw?

Du: _____

Zeugin: Der Junge auf dem Fahrrad ist die Hauptstraße entlanggefahren, als das Auto einbog.

Du: _____

Polizei: Did the car driver stop at the stop sign?

Du: _____

Zeugin: Ja, aber ich glaube, er hat das Fahrrad nicht gesehen. Geht es dem Jungen gut?

Du: _____

Polizei: Yes, but the ambulance is still going to take him to hospital now.

Du: _____

12 Verfasse über den Unfall aus Übung 11 einen kurzen Zeitungsbericht. Verwende auch die indirekte Rede!

Yesterday afternoon at 12.30 _____

Lösungen

Unit 1

1
1. a) oval ball, b) referee, c) pitch → rugby
2. a) tennis racket, b) umpire, c) court → tennis
3. a) goal, b) ice, c) stick → ice hockey
4. a) bat, b) helmet → cricket

2 It is not always easy to talk about sport in the English-speaking world – there are so many different words for the same thing. When you play tennis, you hit the ball with a **racket,** when you play **baseball,** you hit the ball with a bat and when you play hockey, you hit the ball with a **stick.** When you play baseball, you run from one **base** to another on a **field,** but you play rugby on a **pitch** and tennis on a **court.** And if you are an athlete, you run **races** on a **track.**
We use the same words to mean different things, too. If you play football in the USA, you wear a **helmet** on the head. Irish football has yet different **rules.**

3 1. skateboarding; 2. sweat; 3. marathon; 4. gold medal; 5. (world) record; 6. skis
→ A sport: **rowing**

4 1. Nomen; 2. Verb; 3. Verb; 4. Nomen

5
1. Her jump is really high.
2. His kick is very hard.
3. Will there be enough snow this year?
4. The rowing boat had a crash.

6 1. a); 2. b); 3. c)

7 1. Ärmelkanal; 2. Sender/(Fernseh-)Kanal; 3. lenken/richten

8 1. to check; 2. to control; 3. to hit

9 **agreeing:** I agree./That's what I think, too./I think, that's true, too.
disagreeing: I don't agree./I don't think that's true./Don't be silly.

10

John: Hi Gemma. How **is it going?**
Gemma: Oh, fine. We**'re just having** a picnic.
John: No, I mean in the game. **Are they playing** well?
Gemma: Oh, the game! I don't know. I **don't understand** it at all. The man **hits** the ball and then sometimes he **runs** and gets points but sometimes he **doesn't run** at all and he gets more points.
John: Gemma. **Don't you know** the rules?
Gemma: Of course not. Girls **don't play** cricket at school.
John: So why did you go?
Gemma: Well, my brother bought the tickets and the picnic and I **love** picnics.

11

Wendy: Look! Yvonne is tired now. Liz **is going to win** the match.
Chris: I don't know. Look at those clouds. We**'re going to have** a storm soon and then they**'ll stop** the match.
Wendy: I hope they **won't stop** the match. Liz only needs to win two more games.
Chris: Did you phone Tim? **Are you going to meet** him later?
Wendy: Yes, I called him. He**'s going to come** here at three and we**'re going to play** tennis. Do you want to play, too?
Chris: Oh, I think I**'ll go** home. I don't want to get wet.

12 1. future; 2. future; 3. present; 4. present

13

Jake: You're going on your skiing holiday on Saturday, aren't you? How **are you going to** get there?
Susan: We**'re going to fly.** The plane **leaves** really early in the morning and so I hope **won't** miss it.
Jake: And what time **do/will you** *(beides möglich)* arrive home again?
Susan: At 8 pm on the next Saturday. I hope I**'ll be** good at skiing by then.
Jake: Well, I hope you **won't break** your leg on the first day.
Susan: No, I won't. The plane **arrives** at 10 o'clock but then we have to get on a coach so we **won't** arrive until about 4 o'clock.

14

What are you doing at the weekend?
I'm playing football on Saturday.
Pete is going skateboarding on Sunday.
We're watching the cricket.

15

1.
Boy: I'm going to a hockey match tomorrow evening. What are you doing?
Girl: I'm meeting Tina.

2.
Girl: Where's Chris?
Boy: He's at the tennis club. He's playing tennis with some mates.
3.
Boy: You're in a hurry. Where are you going?
Girl: I'm going to my athletics club. Do you want to come?
Boy: No, some friends are coming to my house at 8 pm.

1. a) future, b) future; 2. present; 3. a) present, b) present, c) future

16 *Tim:* **Are you going** to Brighton for the marathon tomorrow?
Mike: Yes, **I am. I'm going** by bus. Do you want to come with me? The bus **leaves** at twelve.
Tim: What time **does the bus arrive?**
Mike: It **arrives** about 12.30.
Tim: That's very early. The marathon **doesn't start** until three o'clock.
Mike: Yes, but I**'m meeting** Pete at one so we can get warm first.
Tim: Why do you want to get warm first?
Mike: Didn't you know? We**'re running** in the marathon.

17 I can't ski. – I'll teach you.
I'm so cold. – I'll lend you my jacket.
I know the way. – Will you show me?
These ski boots are too small. – I'll get you a bigger size.
You don't have enough money. – Will you lend me some?

18 1.
Boy: I've got two tickets for the baseball match but I don't know anybody who wants to come with me.
Boy: Oh, I'll come with you.
2.
Girl: Oh, I'm really nervous about the tennis match. I'm playing really badly at the moment.
Girl: Oh, I'm sure you'll win.
3.
Girl: Let's meet on Saturday morning.
Boy: No, I play football with my friends then.
4.
Girl: Hey, you're great at skateboarding.
Boy: Thanks.
Girl: And that trick looks really good. Will you teach it to me?
Boy: Yes, OK.
5.
Boy: Oh no. My skis are broken.

Woman: Don't worry. I'll buy you some new ones.

6.
Girl: Which sports do you usually do?
Boy: I run in the 100 metres.

7.
Girl: You can't enter the competition. You have to be over 12.
Boy: I'll be 13 next Friday.

1. Oh, I**'ll come** with you. (spontane Entscheidung)
2. Oh, I'm sure, you**'ll** win.
3. No, I **play** football with my friends then.
4. **Will you teach** it to me? (spontane Entscheidung)
5. I**'ll buy** you some new ones. (spontane Entscheidung)
6. I **run** in the 100 metres.
7. I**'ll be** 13 next Friday.

19
1. I'll lend you my skateboard.
2. I practise every evening.
3. I'm sure you'll win.

20
Tim: We**'re playing** cricket at six but we need more players.
Mike: Oh, I**'ll play** with you. I like cricket.
Tim: OK. Well, we**'re meeting** at six in the park so I**'ll see** you there. And **are you going** to the cricket match tomorrow, too?
Mike: I don't know. What time **does it start?**
Tim: It **starts** at ten and **finishes** about five.
Mike: Well, I can't go until one. I**'m having** a skiing lesson.
Tim: A skiing lesson? But I'm sure it **won't snow** before then.
Mike: No, I know but I**'m going** to the new ski centre and it's inside.

21 1. which; 2. which; 3. who; 4. which; 5. who

22
1. I borrowed some skis which were too small.
2. I paid for a lesson with a teacher who was terrible.
3. I went skiing down a hill which was very scary.

23 Golf is a sport **which** is very popular in England but it is not a sport ~~that~~ most people think is very exciting. In fact there are people **who** think that golf isn't a sport at all because they think of old people **who** walk slowly around a big field or two and every ten minutes or so hit a ball. I was once one of those people. I'm a person **who** loves most sport but I thought that golf was very boring. How wrong I was! A friend ~~who~~ I've known for years and loves golf bought me a lesson for my birthday. It was a present ~~which~~ I didn't really want but you can't say no, can you? And I'm glad I didn't say,

"No, thank you," because it was one of the best presents **that** I've ever had. I loved the lesson and I've loved golf ever since. It's great fun when you play with people ~~who~~ you like and it keeps you fit. You often walk ten kilometres or more around golf courses **which** are very hilly while you are carrying a bag **which** is very heavy.

24 1. –; who; 2. which, which; 3. –

25 People **who** become very good at sport have to train very hard for many years. It helps if they have a sports club **which** is good in their area. And it's always easier for children **whose** friends like sport, too. There are also people **who** have bodies **which** are better for one sport or another. For example, people **whose** legs are longer are often better at running. And, of course, for some sports it's easier for children **whose** parents can buy them good equipment or lessons.

26
1. Hey. Is that the boy whose brother is in our class?
2. Do you know anybody who's really good at skateboarding?
3. There are some football clubs whose players do a lot of work with children.
4. We have a neighbour who's a famous athlete.

1. whose; 2. who's; 3. whose; 4. who's

27
1. The tennis player (who) I wrote to went to my school./The tennis player to whom I wrote went to my school.
2. I've kept the letter (which) he answered my questions in./I've kept the letter in which he answered my questions.
3. He sent me an old racket (which) he once played with./He sent me an old racket with which he once played.
4. He's the tennis star (who) we are now all waiting for./He's the tennis star for whom we are now all waiting.
5. We're having a lesson from the nicest tennis star (who) I have ever heard of./We're having a lesson from the nicest tennis star of whom I have ever heard.

28
1. That's the swimming pool in which the Olympic swimmers will swim.
2. He's an athlete about whom we'll hear a lot.
3. That's the road on which they will run the marathon.
4. Here are some runners to whom everybody will want to talk.

29
1. That's the tennis racket with which I won my first game./That's the tennis racket (which) I won my first game with.

2. That's the player with whom I often practised./That's the player (who) I often practised with.
3. That the journalist to whom I gave my first interview./That's the journalist (who) I gave my first interview to.
4. That's the boy whose father taught me to play.

30 1. cricket; 2. baseball; 3. ice hockey

31 1. 11; 2. white; 3. English-speaking countries; 4. 9; 5. hardball; 6. 4000 years old; 7. cold

32 This game is slow but it isn't easy/is hard to understand.
Players score runs when they run to all four bases.
People all over the world play this game.

33 Two teams which have eleven players each kick the ball and try to score goals. It is a very old game and people who lived in many different countries played the game. People think that modern football started in England.

34 1. Yes, look at Henry go on the outside. He's only got 50 metres to go. Yes, he's going to win it. Is it going to be a new world record? Yes, yes. 43.1 seconds. He's broken the world record in the 400 metres. What a race!
2. Fifteen – love. Williams is playing very well at the moment. Oh, wait a minute. Is there something wrong with her racket? Yes, she's getting a new one. Well, of course, they always bring five or six rackets with them and it sometimes happens that one breaks.
3. Wow! What a hit! He really hit the ball well and he's going … first base, second base … Is he going to make it all the way round? Yes, he's done it.

1. athletics/400 metres; 2. the world record; 3. tennis; 4. her racket; 5. baseball; 6. bases

35 Yes, he's **going** to **win** it. Is it going to **be** a new world record?
He's broken the **world** record in the 400 metres.

36 *(Die Lösung kann je nach Sprecher individuell unterschiedlich ausfallen; hier ist nur die Lösung für den CD-Text wiedergegeben.)*
I'm not‿an‿athlete but‿I‿love‿unusual sports.
I‿love skateboarding‿in the park and surfing‿on‿the sea.
I'm not very‿good‿at sport but I enjoy‿it.
I've had lots‿of‿accidents‿of course, but‿I've never broken‿anything.

37

Ann: Oh, Sally, I don't understand it. Why can't girls play football at our school? It isn't fair.
Sally: But, Ann, no other girls want to play football.
Ann: That's not true. I know lots of other girls who want to play football.
Sally: OK. Well most girls don't want to play football. Football's a sport which is hard and dangerous – just like boys.
Ann: Rubbish. Hockey's much harder than football and we have to play that. I hate it. There's always some girl who hits my legs with her stick and that hurts much more than somebody's foot.
Sally: That's because you're so fast. That's the only way the other players can stop you.
Ann: Oh, don't be silly. Sometimes players want to stop me, but most of the time they just can't control their stick. Susan even hit me on the head with her stick once. But anyway football's just so much more fun than hockey.
Sally: Yes, I agree with you. It's much more fun to watch when men play it. They always have great legs.
Ann: Oh, Sally. You're boy mad.
Sally: And women just aren't as good as men. They haven't got the skill.
Ann: Yes, you're right. And why? Because most girls can't play it at school.
Sally: Well, why don't you ask one of the sports teachers if you can start a team? I'm sure they'll help you. Then you can put some signs on the walls around school and see how many girls come. And then you'll know how many girls are interested.
Ann: That's a good idea. I'll go now. Will you come with me?
Sally: I will if you go and see Mr Simon. He's really nice.
Ann: Oh, Sally. He's a teacher.

1. **c)** passt am besten.
2. But, Ann, no other girls want to play football. – That's not true.
Football's a sport which is hard and dangerous. – Rubbish.
That's the only way the other players can stop you. – Oh, don't be silly.
… football's just so much more fun than hockey. – Yes, I agree with you.
They haven't got the skill. – Yes, you're right.
3. a) false; b) true; c) true; d) true; e) false; *Korrektur:* a) Ann thinks that hockey is more dangerous than football. e) Sally has the idea to start a football team.

Unit 2

1 1. fortress; 2. prison; 3. factory; 4. tower

2 Queen Victoria's **reign** began in 1837 and ended in 1901 when she died. This time is now called the Victorian **Age** and it was an important time in British history.
When Victoria came to the **throne,** the British **Empire** was still very big although the American **colonies** had already become **independent.** The colonies made Britain very rich because they gave Britain cheap raw **materials** and food. The **Industrial** Revolution had already begun and this also helped to make Britain richer still. The Industrial Revolution started because lots of new **inventions** like the steam **engine** meant that people could make things very fast in factories. It made Britain rich but its factories also made lots of people poorer. People who had worked at home now had to work in the factories and live in **slums.**

3 1. Empress; 2. Protestant; 3. servant; 4. knight; 5. Saxon; 6. farmer; 7. Norman; 8. lord
→ Queen Victoria became the **great-grandmother** of many kings and queens.

4 wax – candles; gold – jewellery; steel – steam engines; wood – tables

5 "What is William of Normandy doing now?" **wondered** King Harold. "Do you think we can beat him now?" he asked.
"No, we need more rest," **replied** a knight. King Harold looked angry and looked at the other knights. They looked at the floor. "The men have just walked all the way from the north. They need a rest," **continued** the first knight.
King Harold didn't want to hear any more and he took out a knife.
"You've … you've killed me," **gasped** the knight.
"Well, now you can have a nice long rest," **joked** King Harold.

6 old-fashioned – modern; dirty – clean; expensive – free; strange – normal; question – reply; far – close

7 to attack; to continue; to reply; to suggest; to prepare

8 How about a trip to London?
We could go and see the Globe Theatre.
I suggest we go by Tube.
Shall I get the timetable?

9 1. I can understand the actors there very well.
2. We needn't sit in our seats all the time.
3. You must buy a ticket.
4. We mustn't/can't take photos.
5. You may/can walk around.

10 must – have to
can *(können)* – be able to
needn't – not have to
be able to – can
not have to – needn't
can *(dürfen)* – be allowed to
have to – must
mustn't – not be allowed to
be allowed to – can/may
may – be allowed to

11 1. b); 2. a); 3. c)

12 1. Elizabeth **was able to speak** five languages.
2. Drake **was allowed to attack** the Spanish.
3. Drake **wasn't allowed to keep** all the gold.
4. Elizabeth **didn't have to go** to the theatre.
5. The theatre **had to come** to her.

13 We've had a great holiday and lots of things have been different. Usually when we buy things in the shops, we needn't think too hard but here we**'ve had to** try hard to understand people. Usually we can understand everything on TV but we **haven't been able to** in England. Usually we must go to bed early but on holiday we **haven't had to** go to bed before 11 pm. And usually we can't get up late – our mother doesn't let us stay in bed after 7 am – but on holiday we**'ve been allowed to** stay in bed until lunchtime. But, of course, on holiday we've wanted to get up early.

14 I'll be able to come home when I want to.
I'll be allowed to cook the food which I want to eat.
But maybe I won't be able to cook it?

I won't have to do any homework but I will have to go to work.
I won't be allowed to go to school any more. What a pity!

15
1. I **visited** the Globe Theatre because I**'d heard** that it was interesting.
2. We **bought** some tickets for a play after we**'d visited** the theatre.
3. When we **saw** the play, I**'d never read** a book by Shakespeare.
4. The play **had started** when we **arrived** at the theatre.
5. After I**'d seen** the play, I **wanted** to become an actress.

16
1. The bus **had (already) left** when she **got to** the bus stop.
2. The play **had (already) started** before she **arrived** at the theatre.
3. The Tower of London **had (already) closed** when she **thought** about it.

17
The Romans **had defeated** a lot of Europe and North Africa when they **attacked** England for the second time. They **built** Hadrian's Wall after they **had fought** the Scots for years. When the Romans **left** England, they **had built** many roads and fine buildings. As soon as the Romans **had left,** other people **attacked** England. Later everybody forgot what they **had learnt** from the Romans.

18
→ Zusammenfassung **b)** ist richtig.

19
1. true; 2. false; 3. not in the text; 4. true; 5. false; 6. not in the text
Korrektur: 2. Elizabeth didn't like the trains because they were loud, noisy and dirty. 5. Sam found Elizabeth's father in a church./Sam found Elizabeth in a factory's garden.

20
1. c); 2. c); 3. b); 4. a)

21
1. "You can't look after me." (l. 14)
2. I had been to Manchester last year but everything was different now. (l. 37)
3. The driver saw me and said that I could go in and have a look. (l. 46)
4. She gave me some food from the garden and she told me that she could read and write now. (l. 73)

22
(*Die Lösung kann je nach Sprecher individuell unterschiedlich ausfallen; hier ist nur die Lösung für den CD-Text wiedergegeben.*)
The Romans weren't able to keep the Scots out of England so they built Hadrian's Wall.
King Harold's army had had to walk for miles before they fought the battle against William of Normandy.
Queen Elizabeth the First was a very popular queen for a long time but at the end the people became unhappy with her.

23

Mother: Where have you been? Why are you back so late from your day trip to London?
Calvin: Oh mum. I've had a terrible day. You won't believe it when I tell you what happened.
Mother: Why, what happened? Did you get lost?
Calvin: No, I didn't. I stayed with my class and we visited the Tower of London.
Mother: Oh, was it interesting?
Calvin: Yes, it was really interesting. We saw the Great Tower but the most interesting part was the dungeons. But we'd just got there when I needed to go to the toilet so I went to find one. When I got back to the dungeons, I couldn't find my class. They had already left. I looked in some more dungeons and then I found a door which looked interesting. I opened the door and went in. I hadn't found the light when the door closed behind me. I shouted, "Help. Let me out," but nobody opened the door. I was scared and I didn't know what to do. I shouted again and then I heard a noise. I waited for the door to open but it didn't open. Then I saw a light and a head. It was a ghost's head. I wanted to run away but I couldn't move my legs because I was so scared. But then the ghost said, "Follow me. I'll show you how to get out." I followed her upstairs and downstairs and through some doors and then she pointed at a white door. "You can get out there," she said. I looked at the door and when I looked back, she had gone. I went through the door and came out outside the White Tower. I didn't feel very good so I sat down and when I had had a drink and a sandwich, I felt better. I'd just stood up again when my teacher came round the corner. He was very angry. He thought that I'd sat there all the time and that I wasn't interested. It wasn't fair. I told him what had happened, but he didn't believe me.
Mother: Calvin. That was a great story but now tell me what really happened.
Calvin: Oh, Mum.

richtige Reihenfolge: 2 – 5 – 7 – 1 – 3 – 4 – 6 – 8

24

part 1:
Mary: So what should we do at the weekend?
Tom: Well, how about a trip to London? We could go to the Science Museum.
Mary: That's a good idea. I'd really like to go on the London Eye and I'd love to see the Tower of London.
Jean: Oh, but that's so expensive.
Mary: Yes, I know, but it's really interesting and you can spend all day in the Tower.

Jean:	OK. Well, let's go to London then but how should we get there?
Mary:	We can go by train. Shall I get a timetable?
Tom:	No, we can look on the Internet and we can buy the tickets right away, too.
Mary:	OK. Let's do that. And why don't we check what's on at the theatre, too? Maybe we can get some tickets now.
Tom:	Good idea. But shouldn't we ask our parents first?
Mary:	Yes, that's a good idea. Maybe they'll give us some money.

part 2:

Mary:	Excuse me. How much are the tickets, please?
Woman:	Well, which play would you like to see?
Mary:	We'd like to see Romeo and Juliet this afternoon, please.
Woman:	Well, let me see. We've got some tickets at 33 pounds.
Mary:	Oh, that's expensive. Are there special prices for children?
Woman:	It's cheaper if you're under 16. But we also have tickets which cost five pounds if you want to stand.
Mary:	Oh, that's a good idea. Yes, can I have three tickets, please? And where can I get a brochure, please?
Woman:	You can get some in that shop over there. And that'll be 15 pounds for the tickets, please.
Mary:	Here you are. Are we allowed to take photos in the theatre?
Woman:	No, the actors don't like that but there are lots of good photos in the brochures there.
Mary:	OK, thank you.

Excuse me. – part 2
Well, how about a trip to London? – part 1
And where can I get a brochure, please? – part 2
Are we allowed to take photos in the theatre? – part 2
How much are the tickets, please? – part 2
And why don't we check what's on at the theatre, too? – part 1
We could go to the Science Museum. – part 1
Yes, that's a good idea. – part 1
… how should we get there? – part 1
We'd like to see Romeo and Juliet this afternoon, please. – part 2
Shall I get a timetable? – part 1
Are there special prices for children? – part 2

25 They want to go to London by **train.**
They want to buy some tickets for the **train** on the Internet.
They buy **three** tickets which cost **five** pounds at the theatre.
They **mustn't** take photos in the theatre.

Revision A (Unit 1–2)

1
1. This is something which you can wear: jewellery
2. This is a woman who has an empire: empress
3. These are things which everybody needs and swimmers need big ones: lungs
4. This is something which you need when you want to play tennis: racket
5. This is something which a queen or king sits on: throne
6. This is a person who can run, throw or jump: athlete
7. These are things which swimmers or ski jumpers wear: goggles
8. This is a woman who is married to a lord: lady
9. This is a person who lives in a rich person's house and works for them: servant
10. This is a country which has to give its raw materials to another country: colony

2
open a new building; control your speed; flap your arms; attack an enemy; feed a horse; clean a house; nod your head; continue a journey

3
I've just seen a game of American football. Somebody gave me a **free** ticket, so I went to the match. It's an **unusual** game in England and I'd never seen a match before, so I was excited. They played it with an **oval** ball, like rugby. But it's more **modern** than rugby – people have played rugby for a long time. I'm surprised how many people were interested in the game – I'm sure, there were over 1000 there, although I don't know the **exact** number. And they all wanted to have a **close** look at this strange game. It wasn't bad but I don't believe it'll ever become popular.

4
I'm meeting Albert again tomorrow. I love him and we've already planned everything. First we**'re going to** travel on a train. I'm so excited. I've never been on a train before. I hope I **won't be** scared. Then we**'re watching** a horse race. The horse race **starts** at three o'clock and I hope that I **won't** miss the first race. One of my horses **is going to** start in it and he**'ll probably** win – he's a great horse. I'd like to ride a horse, too, but I can't, of course. Women can't do things like that. When I'm Queen, **I'll change** all that. Yes, my uncle is ill and he**'s going to die** soon. Then **I'll be** Queen. Queen Victoria. Sounds good, doesn't it?

Lösungen **A**

5
1. When I **saw** the poster, I **had just learnt** some new tricks.
2. The competition **had started** when I **arrived.**
3. I **had practised** for two minutes when I **broke** my skateboard.
4. After **I'd borrowed** a skateboard, I **won** the competition.

6
1. Queen Elizabeth was a queen (who) most English people liked.
2. She was a queen whose pirates stole treasure from the Spanish.
3. Mexico was a country which had lots of gold and silver.
4. Mexico was a country from which Spain brought the treasure.
5. England was a country (which) Spain attacked.

7 I didn't enjoy being Queen. I **wasn't allowed to** do what I wanted and I **had to** be nice to people. I **was allowed to** learn lots of things but I **was never able to** ride a horse. I **didn't have to** worry about money but I **wasn't allowed to** spend it all. No, that wasn't a great job.

8
Mutter: Frag ihn bitte, was die Eintrittskarten kosten.
Du: **How much are the tickets, please?**
Mann: Oh, it's free.
Du: **Der Eintritt ist umsonst.**
Mutter: Das ist ja schön. Können wir auch ins 3D-Kino gehen?
Du: **Great. Can we go in the 3D cinema, too?**
Mann: Yes, but you have to buy a ticket for that.
Du: **Ja, aber dafür müssen wir eine Eintrittskarte kaufen.**
Mutter: OK. Frag ihn, wo wir eine Broschüre über das Museum kaufen können.
Du: **Where can we get a brochure about the museum, please?**
Mann: I've got one here. Here you are.
Mutter: Oh. Thank you. Ähm, dürfen wir hier Fotos machen?
Du: **May we/Can we/Are we allowed to take photos here?**
Mann: You're allowed to take photos in some rooms. You can see signs there.
Du: **Ja, in manchen Räumen. Es stehen Schilder dort.**
Mutter: Gut. Kannst du ihn fragen, wie wir zum Café kommen?
Du: **Can you tell us the way to the café, please?**
Mann: Yes, it's over there, but you can also have picnics here in the museum.
Du: **Es ist dort drüben, aber man kann auch hier im Museum picknicken.**

9
Susan: So how was the game? Did you win?
Mike: I don't know.
Susan: What do you mean you don't know?
Mike: Well, they were still arguing about it when I had to leave. It was the strangest game I've ever played.

A Lösungen

Susan: Why? What happened?
Mike: Well, not much in the first half. We played better but we just couldn't get a goal.
Susan: Well, what's new there?
Mike: Ha ha. Anyway. We'd just come back on the pitch again after half-time when one of their players got the ball and ran the wrong way with it.
Susan: The wrong way?
Mike: Yeah, the wrong way! He just didn't notice. He'd kicked the ball at the goal when he noticed his goal-keeper was standing in it. Anyway the goal-keeper couldn't stop it.
Susan: So that was one – nil to you.
Mike: Yep. But we were still laughing when they scored another goal – for them this time.
Susan: So that was one – one.
Mike: Yep. And the game was really exciting from then on. But there were no more goals until we scored another one after we'd played for about ninety minutes.
Susan: So that was 2 – 1. You won.
Mike: Yes – and no.
Susan: What?
Mike: Well, the referee's watch had stopped. And the game was so exciting that nobody even looked at the time for another ten minutes.
Susan: So what difference does it make?
Mike: Well, we don't know if we scored before the end of the game or not.
Susan: But if the referee hadn't stopped the game then you scored before the end, didn't you? That's it. Two – one.
Mike: That's what we said but the other team said it's not fair and we should have another match.
Susan: And? What do you think?
Mike: Oh, I think we should play again. I just love football.

richtige Reihenfolge: 4 – 2 – 1 – 3 – 5

10 Venus and Serena Williams are sisters who are famous tennis champions. Their father was the man who taught them to play tennis. Before they went to the tennis court, their father watched a video on which he found lots of tips.
The Williams' family grew up in an area of Los Angeles which was very poor. Their father wanted them to do well at sport so that they could have a better life. They worked hard and they had already won lots of matches before they were even 14 years old.

Unit 3

1   1. selfish; 2. jealous; 3. difficult; 4. grumpy; 5. wise

2   I cannot **tell** a lie. James **drives** me crazy. I don't know if I love him or hate him. When I know that I will see him, I **get** dressed very carefully. I think I like him and I think he likes me, too. I'll have to **make** sure or I will **go** crazy. OK. I've **made** a decision. I'm going to ask him out … Or maybe not! Help!

3   a) curtain; b) stage; c) props; d) actor/actress; e) audience; f) lights

4   We **put on** a play last week at school. It was great fun but very hard work. We wrote the play ourselves and it was only short but we still had to **rehearse** a lot. First we all had to learn our parts and then we had about ten **rehearsals** with all the **cast.** My friends were the actors and actresses and I was the **director** because I can't act at all. We didn't need **costumes** because the play was about life at school. It was a funny play – or we thought so anyway. We weren't quite sure if everybody else thought it was funny until the audience **applauded** at the end. Then we knew that everybody else enjoyed it, too.

5   I'm going to split **up** with Lucy tomorrow. We don't get **on** any more. She doesn't listen **to** me and she never turns **off** the TV. I will turn **into** a couch potato if I stay with her. Tomorrow I'm going to put **on** my best clothes, eat **up** my dinner and then tell her. I feel sorry **for** her, of course, but you know; that's life. And anyway I'm going to go out **with** her best friend when I've called her.

6

w	t	u	l	a	w	w	i	s	h
e	r	d	e	c	i	d	e	o	u
m	a	n	a	g	e	d	s	k	n
a	n	t	v	h	z	x	r	m	e
r	s	f	e	l	r	a	n	a	a
r	l	q	s	t	a	n	d	w	r
y	a	b	v	l	d	r	b	h	n
j	t	c	o	n	t	a	c	t	i
b	e	h	a	v	e	f	q	u	j
k	e	u	a	y	s	c	h	a	t

erreichen – contact; ertragen – stand; verdienen – earn; schaffen – manage; hinterlassen – leave; übersetzen – translate; heiraten – marry; sich benehmen – behave; entscheiden – decide; wünschen – wish; plaudern – chat

7 You've got a point, but …
That's true, but …
I don't mind that, but …
I know, but …
I guess you're right, but …

8 1. I'm just calling to say I'll be home late.
2. Could you call me back, please?
3. Can I take a message?
4. Can you spell it for me, please?
5. Hope to hear from you soon.
6. I'd like to speak to Chris.

9 Es eignen sich die Sätze **1, 2, 5.**

10 I've just hurt **myself.**
Bye everybody! I hope you all enjoyed **yourselves.**
She often talks to **herself.**
They made that CD **themselves.**
Jane! Remember to behave **yourself** at your grandma's.

11 It was Friday. I got up and then got dressed ~~myself~~ as always. I was late and had to hurry ~~myself~~, as always. I went to school, worked hard and behaved myself – as always! I got home, sat down ~~myself~~ and relaxed ~~myself~~ – as always. My dad made dinner and hurt himself with a knife – as always. I ate dinner and got ready ~~myself~~ for youth club – as always – on a Friday! When I got to youth club, I met ~~myself~~ a girl. We laughed and enjoyed ourselves. I felt ~~myself~~ happy – as always. But nothing now was as always – everything had changed ~~itself~~.

12 Did you really make it yourselves?
John wrote it himself.
I don't want to ask him myself.
You have to find it yourself.
Can we cook dinner ourselves?

13 1. Hey. Stop it! You're going to hurt yourself.
2. Well, thank you for coming. Have you enjoyed yourselves?
3. Isn't that picture good? Do you think he drew it himself?
4. She's really good at music. She taught herself to play the piano, you know?
5. No, we want to do it ourselves.
6. They tidied their room themselves.

1. yourself → reflexiv
2. yourselves → reflexiv
3. himself → verstärkend
4. herself → reflexiv
5. ourselves → verstärkend
6. themselves → verstärkend

14 We wrote the play ourselves.
Everybody got ready.
We had to hurry up.
I was the director and I couldn't relax.
But everybody enjoyed themselves.

15 1. They met **each other.**
2. They looked at **themselves.**
3. They looked at **each other.**
4. They taught **themselves** to build a boat.
5. They took photos of **each other.**

16 If my sister's boyfriend asks her, she'll marry him.
My dad won't be happy if she marries him soon.
If they marry, my sister will leave home.
If my sister leaves home, I'll have my own room. Hurray.
Will I be happy if I have my own room?

17 If my dad **was** rich, we could live in a big house. If we lived in a big house with a garden, I**'d have** my own horse. If our house **had** lots of rooms, I **wouldn't have to** share a room with my sister. I **would buy** more clothes if I had more money. If my dad was rich, my parents **wouldn't have to** work. If my parents **didn't work,** they might stay at home all day. Yuk! I'm glad my dad isn't rich.

18 I'll have my party at my sport's club if they let me.
If I invite all my friends, will they all come?
If we had a big house, all my friends could come here.
We could have a party in the garden if my birthday was in summer.
If my dad gives me money, I'll save it for a holiday.
I'd make a cake if I could cook well.
If I ask my brother, will he bring his friends?

19 Our house is small. If we **had** more rooms, I think we**'d fight** less. For example, we **wouldn't have** the same problems in the morning if we **had** more bathrooms. My brother is 18 soon and he wants to go to Spain for a year. If he **goes** to Spain, we**'ll have** more room at home, but I**'ll miss** him. If he **likes** it, he **may** stay there. If he **stays** there, maybe I**'ll be able to** stay with him but maybe he **won't invite** me. If we all **lived** in Spain, we **wouldn't need** a big house because we**'d be able** to live outside more. I'd like that.

20 If I hadn't watched the late film, I would have got up earlier.
If I'd got up earlier, I would have gone to London with my friends.
If I'd gone to London, I would have met my favourite actor, too.
He might have spoken to me if I'd met him.

21 My parents went out last night. If my parents **hadn't gone** out, I **wouldn't have invited** my friends. Joanne's cousins were staying with her over the weekend. If they **hadn't been** at her house, she **wouldn't have brought** them with her. If she **hadn't brought** her cousins, they **couldn't have broken** my mum's favourite clock. It's Sunday today. If it **was** Saturday, I**'d look for** a new clock for my mother. I've got an idea: I could try to mend it. If I mend it well, she **won't know** that they broke it – maybe. Oh no. They're coming. I know, if I **hide** it, she **won't see** it and I'll be able to buy a new one tomorrow. What a pain! If my parents **go out** next weekend, I**'ll stay** at home alone!

22 The play wouldn't have been as good if you hadn't worked hard. If I were you, I'd audition for another play.

23 Scene 1: c); Scene 2: a); Scene 3: b)

24 1. b); 2. a); 3. a); 4. c); 5. b); 6. c)

25 1. a); 2. b); 3. c); 4. a)

26
x X:	behave, decide, myself
X x:	frozen, marry, selfish
x X x:	decision, especially, reflexive
X x x:	answerphone, microwave, probably

27
Mum: Can we talk about last night?
Nic: Yeah. If we have to.
Mum: We agreed that you'd be home at 10 o'clock. You didn't …
Nic: We didn't agree on a time. You decided! And that's not fair. I'm fourteen, Mum. All my friends can stay out until 12 o'clock and I have to be home at 10 on a Saturday. That's not fair.
Mum: I know, but I'm not your friends' mum. I am your mum and you need enough sleep.
Nic: But I can sleep late on Sunday and still have enough sleep.
Mum: Well, you've got a point, but I was very worried about you last night. I didn't know where you were. And that's not fair.
Nic: I guess you're right but can't we meet halfway? Can't I stay out later at the weekend? And if we agree on a time, I won't be late again.
Mum: OK, fine. I'll let you stay out later on Saturday if do all your homework first.
Nic: OK, great. Er. And Mum …
Mum: Yes.
Nic: Can I go out tonight?

Can we talk about last night?
We agreed that you'd be home at 10 o'clock.
I know, but I'm not your friends' mum.
Well, you've got a point, but I was very worried about you last night.
I guess you're right but can't we meet halfway?
I'll let you stay out later on Saturday if do all your homework first.

28 **Phone call 1:**
Ann's Mum: This is 736 8243. Hello.
Kylie: Hi. Here's Kylie. Is Ann there?
Ann's Mum: No, she isn't here. She isn't back from tennis club yet.
Kylie: Oh, could you ask her to call me back, please?
Ann's Mum: Yes, of course. She should be back in a minute. Should she call you at home or your mobile?

3 Lösungen

Kylie: Oh, at home. I'm trying to do my Maths homework and I just can't do it.
Ann's Mum: Oh OK. Well, I don't think she's done her homework yet but I'll tell her.

a) to Ann, b) at the tennis club, c) call her back

Phone call 2:
Answering machine: Sorry, we can't answer the phone at the moment. If you'd like to leave a message after the tone, we'll call you back.
Diana: Hi. This is Diana. I'm just calling to say I can't go to the cinema this evening. I'm going to be home late. Maybe we can go tomorrow. Can you call me back tomorrow morning, please? Thanks. See you.

a) Diana, b) She can't go to the cinema tonight. c) tomorrow morning

Phone call 3:
Neil: Hello.
Man: Hello. This is Tariq Kumar. I'd like to speak to your dad, please.
Neil: Oh, I'm afraid he isn't in at the moment. Can I take a message?
Man: Yes, please. Could you tell him that I called and could he call me back, please?
Neil: Yes. Just a moment. I'm sorry, I didn't understand your name. Could you spell it for me, please?
Man: Yes, of course. It's Tariq Kumar. That's T – A – R – I – Q Kumar, K – U – M – A – R.
Neil: OK, I've got that. Does my dad have your phone number?
Man: Yes, I think so but I'll give it to you again. It's 0162 245 7634.
Neil: Er. 0162 245 7634.
Man: Yes, that's right. Thanks a lot.
Neil: You're welcome. Goodbye.

a) Tariq Kumar, b) 0162 245 7634, c) call him back

Unit 4

1 The northwest of England is famous for its **industry** – the Industrial Revolution started here – but it is also a beautiful **region.** Away from the cities the **landscape** is wild with many mountains and lakes and it's perfect for many **leisure** activities like rock climbing. Even the cities are beautiful and interesting. Manchester has had a **facelift** recently and Liverpool's **waterfront** is a must-see. Around the area you can still see lots of signs of the **heavy industry** which was once so important here, for example, you can still see **coal mines** although they are not used any more. Now many new smaller **firms** have started in the area; more people work in high-tech or leisure industries now. The area has changed and left its past behind.

2 Wales – Welsh; Punjab – Punjabi; Asia – Asian; Scotland – Scottish; Italy – Italian; America – American

3 1. riechen – to smell; klingen – to sound; aussehen – to look; fühlen – to feel; schmecken – to taste
2. duften – to smell, hören – to hear; schauen – to look; sich anfühlen – to feel; scheinen – to seem

4 I'd love to **try out** those new skateparks.
A skater did a great trick and everybody **cheered.**
We're going to **move** to Cardiff.
Not much heavy industry **exists** there now.

5 My cousin is very proud **of** his job. He helps bands at their shows and he's always **on** the move. He's really **into** music so he loves it and although he has to work really hard, he never gets tired **of** it. We always make fun **of** him because he often hangs **out** with these famous people, but he doesn't mind – he wants to be in a band, too, one day.

6

d	t	a	s	t	e	q	m	e	f
c	g	p	r	e	g	i	o	n	e
r	b	h	r	j	z	n	t	v	n
o	a	l	e	r	n	a	o	o	g
w	n	c	l	a	f	x	r	z	i
d	l	u	a	s	h	r	w	l	n
b	i	r	t	h	p	l	a	c	e
w	k	r	i	d	g	u	y	k	e
a	x	y	v	f	u	s	b	o	r
t	e	a	e	d	i	n	n	e	r

food: taste, curry, tea, dinner
people: crowd, relative, engineer
places: region, motorway, birthplace

7 regional culture; abstract noun; definite article; bilingual children; weird place

8 1. by; 2. until; 3. until

9
Man: Are you lost? **Can I help you?**
Woman: Yes please. Can you tell me how to get to the waterfront museum?
Man: Yes, I can show you the way if you like.
Woman: **That's very kind of you.**

Girl: I'm terrible sorry if I hurt you yesterday.
Mum: Yes, you did. Never mind if that's what you think.
Girl: **I didn't mean to be rude.**
Mum: **Well, be more careful next time.**

10 I've just moved to Wales and I love it here. It's a **beautiful** place – the mountains and the coastline are lovely – and the people are **friendly.** Most people here speak English and Welsh and I want to learn Welsh, too, although I think it's a **strange** language. Maybe if I work **hard,** I'll be able to understand people soon. When they speak English, they have **strange** accents but I think they speak **beautifully.** It sounds like the people are singing. And many people sing well, too, although not everybody is in a choir, of course.

11   *Sue:*   Is that our carriage?
John: Er … let me just look at **our** tickets. Er … No, it isn't **ours.** We need number 14.
(…)
Man: Excuse me. I think you are sitting in **my** seat.
John: No, I'm sure it's **mine.** Look! Here's **my** ticket. Can I see **your** ticket, please?
Man: Yes, here it is. Look. Seat 56, carriage 13.
John: Oh, but this is carriage 14. **Yours** must be the next one.
(…)
Sue: What a funny day! Look that boy can't find **his** seat now.
John: The seat opposite us is empty. Maybe that's **his.**
Sue: No, that seat is that girl's. Look! That coat is **hers.**
John: Oh yes. Why can't people find **their** seats easily!

12   Does **money make you** happy?
Do you **go to school by** bike?
I **love** music.
My parents don't **like the music** which I like.

13   I like (–) school really but I don't feel so good today and **the** school which I go to is on the other side of town so I really don't want to go today. I usually go by (–) bus, of course and I can't come home for (–) lunch, but that's no problem.
I've got **a** headache, but I don't need to see **the** doctor because my mum's **a** doctor. She says that I'm not ill and I have to go to (–) school. She says I just stayed out too late last night. My mum never lets me stay at home. I wish she was **an** engineer or something and then I could see **a** normal doctor. I went to see **a** band last night. **The** music wasn't very good but **the** singer was wonderful. He's **the** love of my life – well, at **the** moment anyway. I don't need **a** boyfriend but (–) love makes (–) life sweeter, doesn't it? And I love (–) music so it's great to have **a** boyfriend who can sing well.

14   1. The rich aren't always happier than the poor.
4. She doesn't go to a school for the blind.
5. Are the old usually wise?

15   My aunt's got a <u>good</u> job but it isn't always <u>easy</u>. She works <u>hard</u> and for <u>many</u> hours and so she often gets <u>tired</u>. She works with <u>young</u> people so it's <u>good</u> that she's a <u>friendly</u> person. Sometimes people react <u>badly</u> or shout at her <u>angrily</u> but she always stays <u>calm</u>. She likes people and gets on <u>well</u> with most people so she usually feels <u>good</u> about her job. And what is it? She's a teacher.

16 Maria went to Canterbury to learn English. She arrived on Friday evening and walked **slowly** around the town. She thought that it looked **beautiful**. Many of the buildings were **old** and there were lots of **interesting** restaurants and theatres, too. After some time she got **hungry** and decided to try some **good** English food. The first restaurant she found smelt **delicious** but it was French. She found five more restaurants **quickly** but not one of them was English. She asked somebody but she didn't understand the answer because the woman's English sounded **strange.** She was Italian. Then she heard some music in one restaurant and people were talking **happily.** It sounded and smelt **great** and so she went in. It was Irish.

17 My dad drives fast/dangerously/well/happily.
My dad seems dangerous/good/interesting/young/happy.

18 I'll have forgotten everything I learned at school by Monday morning.
My older brother will have left England by Sunday night.
I'll have fought with my sister before the end of the weekend.
I won't have done any schoolwork by the last day of the holidays.
We'll all have swum in the sea.
We won't have got bored before the end of the holidays.

19 *simple present:* b)
present progressive: c)
will future: d), e)
going to future: a), c), g)
future perfect: f)

20 A friend **is moving** house tomorrow. Her train **leaves** at 11 o'clock and **I'm going** to the station with her. Her dad **is going to travel** down with all their things the day after. This time next week she**'ll have started** her new school and she**'ll have made** some new friends.
She doesn't want to leave. She says things are worse for her than for me because she **won't** know anybody there and she**'ll miss** everything here. I think she's wrong. Things **will be** worse for me. Everything **will be** exciting for her. **I'm going to visit** her at Christmas and by then she**'ll have met** lots of new people and done lots of new things. I **won't have done** anything new. There'll just be a hole where she was.

21 1. I'm glad, I needn't wear **glasses.** They're very expensive. My mum's got three **pairs of glasses** and she loses **them** all the time.
2. I don't wear **trousers** very often. I don't like them. I've only got two **pairs of trousers.**
3. I love **dresses.** I've got 15 **dresses.** I even wear **them** at school.
4. My friend loves **shoes.** She's just bought three **pairs of shoes.** She works so that she can buy new **shoes.**

22 William: the Isle of Wight or the Lake District (A or C)
Ellen: Newcastle or Bristol (B or D)
Maria: the Isle of Wight or the Lake District (A or C)
Liam: Newcastle or Bristol (B or D)

23 William: the Lake District (C)
Ellen: Bristol (D)
Maria: Isle of Wight (A)
Liam: Newcastle (B)

24 1. off the south coast of England
2. not very much
3. surfing, windsurfing
4. north of England, near the coast
5. its nightlife
6. football
7. in the northwest of England
8. walk, climb, canoe, sail, swim, dive, enjoy the views
9. wet / it rains a lot
10. Bath, South Wales, Cornwall, Devon, Dorset
11. its music and film industries
12. America

25 1. true; 2. not in the text; 3. false; 4. true; 5. false; 6. not in the text; 7. false;
Korrektur: 3. Not many tourists go to Newcastle. 5. You don't have to be very fit to walk in the Lake Distict. 7. Bristol has an airport.

26 1. weird; 2. quite; 3. smelt; 4. ice; 5. hat

27 *Woman 1:* Those bags look very heavy. Can I help you?
Woman 2: Well, I'm just going home and you're going into town, aren't you?
Woman 1: I'm not in a hurry. So it's no problem. I can take them home for you if you like.
Woman 2: That's very kind of you. Thanks.

Boy 1: She looks nice, doesn't she?
Boy 2: Who? That girl with dark hair?
Boy 1: Yeah. I wish I could talk to her.
Boy 2: Well, go and say hello then.
Boy 1: Yes, I will. (…) Haven't we met before?
Girl: No, I don't think so.

Boy: Hi.
Girl: Hi Richard. How are you?
Boy: OK.

Girl: Look. I'm very sorry about yesterday.
Boy: Don't worry about it.
Girl: I didn't mean to be rude.

1. b); 2 c); 3. b)

28
Luke: Hello.
Jill: Hi. It's me.
Luke: Hi Jill.
Jill: So what was it like?
Luke: It was OK. Brighton's nice. The house was OK. The country around Brighton is beautiful. We're going to live near the sea …
Jill: You'll be able to go swimming before breakfast every day then.
Luke: Yeah, yeah. The school sounds good and I met a few kids who will be in my class. They seemed nice, too.
Jill: Great. You'll love it then.
Luke: I'm sure I will like it. I think Brighton's a really exciting place but I'll miss you, you know?
Jill: Ah, you'll have forgotten me by Christmas.
Luke: I won't. I'll never forget you. Will you come and visit me?
Jill: If you ask me and my Mum says I can go. What can you do in Bristol then?
Luke: Well, the beach is great and they have lots of bands there in summer.
Jill: Oh, that sounds good. When are you moving?
Luke: We're moving at the end of July.
Jill: At the end of July? I thought you wanted to move at the end of August. And I thought you wanted to spend the summer with me.
Luke: Well, I do. You know that. But Mum and Dad want to move sooner so that they can sort everything out before they start work.
Jill: They probably want to enjoy the beach in summer, too.
Luke: Yes, well, why don't you come down and stay in the summer?
Jill: Oh, that would be great. I could come down in August for your birthday.
Luke: Er, well, not for my birthday. I'm meeting some of the kids from my new school, who I met when I went down.
Jill: Oh. Well, that's nice.
Luke: Yes, well, they asked me to a party. And Lisa's parents have got a swimming pool in the garden.
Jill: Lisa? Who's Lisa?
Luke: She's just a girl in my class. There'll be lots of boys there, too.
Jill: Yes, I am sure there will be. Well, have a good time, Luke.

Lösung: b)

29 1. a); 2. c); 3. b); 4. c); 5. b)

Revision B (Unit 3–4)

1 ein Risiko eingehen – to take a risk
sich anziehen – to get dressed
sich kräuseln – to go curly
eine Entscheidung treffen – to make a decision
sichergehen – to make sure
ausflippen – to go crazy
sich Zeit lassen – to take your time
sich lustig machen über – to make fun of
etwas sattbekommen: to get tired of

2 Caroline won't go **out** with me and I don't know why. Don't you feel sorry **for** me? I'm a really nice guy. I eat **up** my vegetables, turn **off** my mp3 player when teachers are talking and I get **on** with everybody – well, almost. I'm **into** books, music and sport. I'm good **at** school and my parents are proud **of** me. I don't hang **out** with the wrong people. I don't make fun **of** people and I never laugh **at** rude jokes. Well, maybe I'm just too perfect!

3 1. guy *(die anderen sind weiblich)*
2. caller *(die anderen sind Gruppen von Menschen)*
3. vegetarian *(die anderen sind Berufe)*
4. purse *(die anderen kann man essen)*
5. junk *(die anderen sind Kommunikationsmittel)*
6. curtain *(die anderen kann man anziehen)*

4 We all meet twice a week.
Jane taught herself how to put on a play.
Peter makes many props himself.
We all watch ourselves on video after a play.
I can never relax before a play.

5 If I hadn't been to the theatre, I **wouldn't have found out** that I like plays. If I **didn't like** plays, I wouldn't want to be an actor. I wouldn't have known about the audition if I **hadn't seen** the poster. If I don't go to the audition, I **won't know** if I'm good enough – but I'm so scared. My friends ask me why I'm scared. "If you**'re not** good enough, you won't get the part. That's no problem. If you practise more and learn more, you**'ll get** a part some time." If I wasn't so shy, it probably **wouldn't be** a problem. "If most famous actors hadn't done many auditions, they **would never have become** famous," say my friends. I don't think I want to be famous. "Why don't you just be a director?" asked my mum. Oh yes, what a good idea!

6 I**'m going** to Liverpool on Monday. My plane **arrives** at four and I**'m going to stay** with a family for two weeks. I**'ll have met** the family by Monday evening. I hope we**'ll like** each other. I hope by the end of my holiday I**'ll have improved** my English a lot. Well, I'm sure it**'ll be** better than now.

7 Your trousers look good. Did you make them yourself? How many pairs of trousers do you have/have you got now?

8 Last summer I stayed on ~~farm~~ → **a farm** and it was great. ~~The life~~ → **Life** is very different on a farm and it seemed ~~strangely~~ → **strange** at first but I soon got used to it. The parents worked ~~hardly~~ → **hard** every day and they didn't have much time to ~~relax themselves~~ → **relax,** but life was slower on the farm. Nobody seemed to be ~~in hurry~~ → **in a hurry.** The mother usually cooked ~~the lunch~~ → **lunch** and we all ate it together. The food always smelt ~~deliciously~~ → **delicious** and everybody was always hungry after a day outside in the fields. I liked ~~life~~ → **the life** of the farmer so much that I want to be ~~farmer~~ → **a farmer** now. It would be easier if my parents ~~are~~ → **were** farmers, too, but I'll learn even if I have to ~~teach~~ → **teach myself** everything.

9 *Ellis:*   Hello. This is 432 6887.
Woman: Hello, this is Cynthia Wallis here. Can I speak to your mother, please?
Ellis: I'm sorry, she isn't in at the moment. Can I take a message?
Woman: Yes, please. I can't meet her for tennis this evening. Can you ask her to call me back, please?
Ellis: Yes, does she have your number?
Woman: Yes, but wait a minute. When will she be home do you think?
Ellis: Well, at about four o'clock.
Woman: OK. Good. Can you give her my office number then, please? It's four seven two, three double five one.
Ellis: Four, seven, two, three, double five, one. And I'm sorry, I didn't quite understand your name, please.
Woman: It's Cynthia. C – y – n – t – h – i – a. She'll know who I am.

Cynthia Wallis phoned. Her office number is 472 3551. She can't play tennis this evening.

10   *Vater:*   Die Frau dort hat eine schwere Tasche. Frag sie, ob wir ihr helfen können.
Du: **Can we help you?**
Frau: Oh, yes please. That's very kind of you. I'm sorry I can't walk so quickly.
Du: **Sie sagt ja, und das sei sehr nett von uns. Aber es tut ihr leid, sie kann nicht so schnell laufen.**
Vater: Sag ihr, sie soll sich Zeit lassen.
Du: **Take your time.**
(Dein Vater lässt eine Tasche fallen, und etwas geht kaputt.)
Vater: Oh! Sag ihr, dass es mir furchtbar leid tut!
Du: **We're terribly sorry.**
Frau: Don't worry about it. It's no problem.
Du: **Wir sollen uns keine Gedanken machen, es ist nicht schlimm.**

11   *Boy:*   What were you doing yesterday with Paul?
Girl: Nothing. I just met him at the youth club.
Boy: He's Gemma's boyfriend, isn't he?
Girl: Yes, he is, but he's my friend, too.
Boy: He was very close to you. Did he kiss you?
Girl: No, he didn't. But he asked me to go with him.
Boy: Did he? I hope you said no. (…) You didn't say yes, did you?
Girl: No, I didn't. I said I'd think about it. I really don't know what to do.
Boy: What do you mean you don't know what to do? He's your best friend's boyfriend!

→ Das Mädchen heißt **Sophie.**

12   1. false; 2. true; 3. false; 4. false

13   → Die Antwort passt zu dem Brief von **Sophie.**

14   No, don't tell your friend. If you tell her, she'll be angry. If I were you, I'd watch her boyfriend. If you see him with other girls, tell your friend. Don't worry about it. They'll probably split up anyway.

Unit 5

1 **across:** 1. newspap**e**r; 3. popul**a**r; 4. co**n**cert; 8. ad**v**ertisemen**t**; 10. quality
down: 2. soap; 3. progra**m**me; 5. celebri**t**y; 6. head**li**ne; 7. stud**io**; 9. m**e**dia
→ Some people use media more for information and some more for **entertainment.**

2 discover/photograph/cast an actor
rewrite/reread a script
film an ad
sign a contract
advertise a product

3 My **agent,** John, contacted me last night about a **casting.** He sent me the **script** for the film but I didn't really like it. There was too much **violence** for my taste. But it's difficult to get work and John thinks I have the right **look.** The director's **assistant** is going to send me the **sides** tomorrow and I'll learn them before the casting. Then if I'm lucky, I'll have the **contract** in my pocket in a couple of weeks.

4 create: erschaffen; copy: nachahmen; changed: sich verändert; exchange: austauschen

5 Yesterday I was just walking **past** the cinema when somebody on the roof got my **attention.** I saw that it was a boy who was wearing red and blue and just then, he fell **off**. Or did he? I found out that he had jumped off because he thought he was Superman. Anyway he **cut** his leg on some glass on the floor and he also had a big **gash** in his arm. It was bleeding terribly and so I called an **ambulance.** While we were waiting for the ambulance, I **tied** a bandage around the gashes on his arm and leg. I had my sports clothes in my bag and so I used those as **bandages.** The boy was very scared because there was **blood** everywhere and so I tried to **distract** him. First I told him jokes and then I made him paper planes with some paper out of my bag. I had **rescued** him but there was a problem. I used my homework to make the paper planes. I'm very sorry, Mr Ellis, but that's why I haven't got my homework with me!

6

e	w	c	e	l	e	b	r	i	t	y
h	b	y	z	l	c	a	o	u	p	c
e	o	o	f	u	j	k	v	x	a	b
c	o	u	c	h	p	o	t	a	t	o
t	k	t	g	e	v	i	z	t	i	g
q	w	h	f	s	b	c	h	k	e	u
h	o	u	s	e	w	i	f	e	n	y
a	r	d	b	a	g	e	n	t	t	k
y	m	a	s	s	i	s	t	a	n	t

couch potato (m/w); bookworm (m/w); youth (m/w); housewife (w); guy (m); agent (m/w); celebrity (m/w); assistant (m/w); patient (m/w)

7 violent – gewalttätig; basic – grundlegend, einfach; awesome – beeindruckend; main – Haupt-; realistic – realistisch; super – super; smooth – glatt; tight – eng

8
Sue: **Did the casting go** well on Saturday?
Rob: No, it **didn't**. I **was** really nervous. **I've tried** to forget it but I can't because it **was** so embarrassing.
Sue: Maybe you **were** better than you **thought. Have you heard** from the director?
Rob: No, I **haven't,** but **I've just phoned** him and his assistant **said** we may hear tomorrow.

9 **Media** has become more important in the last twenty years or so. → *active*
The first **newspapers** were made thousands of years ago. → *passive*
How much is the **radio** listened to in your house? → *passive*
Many **people** still read books every day. → *active*
TV was first watched in the 1920's. → *passive*
Has **the Internet** ever been used by more people? → *passive*
Have **newspapers** ever been all true? → *active*

10 Many films are made in America.
The radio is listened to everywhere.
Books aren't read as much now.
The Internet is used for almost everything.
Are films often watched in the cinema?

11 Televisions **were first made** not long before 1930 and **were sold** about ten years later. Televisions have changed a lot but they **are still used** to watch films, news and programmes. The pictures on the televisions **have been improved** a lot and now, of course, the films **are listened** to, too. We still watch them in our living room, but now the channel **is usually changed** from the sofa. It **was once thought** that if everybody had a TV, nobody would listen to the radio. That hasn't happened. The radio **is still listened** to.

12 The first Harry Potter book was finished by J. K. Rowling in 1995.
The books have been translated into 65 languages.
The books are read by children and older people.
The books have been made into films.
The scenes were filmed in many different places.
Harry Potter is played by Daniel Radcliffe.

13 Liz had already been offered lots of parts by her sixteenth birthday.
She hopes she'll be given many more roles.
I had never been photographed before my casting.
I'll be photographed a lot in the future.
We think we'll be interviewed a lot now that we are stars.

14 The future of books **is often worried** about by many people. They think that fewer books **will be made** in the future because people will watch more and more TV or because information, for example, **will be downloaded** onto the mobile or the computer when **it is needed.** But is this realistic? Books **have always been read.** Well, almost! Books **had been written/were written** before modern paper **was first made.** Of course, they **weren't bought** by many people because they were too expensive. In the time of the Romans books **were even borrowed** from libraries. People were once worried about the future of the radio but history has shown us that the more different media **are used,** the more important they become.

15 The Internet was first used by the public in the 1990s.
Scientists had used the Internet before then.
A web browser is needed when you want to use the Internet.

16 *personal passive:* John was sent the sides (by the agent).
The sides were sent to John (by the agent).
personal passive: John was given a number at the casting (by the assistant).
A number was given to John at the casting (by the assistant).
personal passive: John was offered his first big role (by the director).
His first big role was offered to John (by the director).

17 1. pp; 2. active; 3. active; 4. pp; 5. passive; 6. pp

18 I was invited to my first celebrity party last night. First we were shown the host's new film and then we were given lots of food and drink. The food was made by some famous French cooks and it tasted delicious. Some great music was played by a band and we were told lots of funny stories. Lots of new friends were made but I wasn't even asked what my name was.

19 **A:** Alan Wisdom Hurt in Fire
B: Violence at Football Match
C: Boy Attacked after School

20
1. Alan Wisdom and two cameramen.
2. At a TV studio in Manchester.
3. In a studio.
4. They were cut by glass from a window.
5. 55 people were hurt.
6. He was hit by a bottle.
7. Six.
8. He was attacked by two youths.
9. In Church Street at about 4:30.
10. Anybody who saw anything.

21 A famous painting has been stolen from the Tate Gallery in London. It is thought that the Monet was stolen about eight o'clock in the evening.
Two men were seen behind the Tate at about 8 o'clock. They were climbing out of a window and they were carrying something. They were both wearing masks and black clothes.
Anybody who saw anything should phone the police on 0208 566 2131.

22 1.
Who's that present **for?**
It's for Ann.
2.
Where do you want to go **to?**
I'd like to go to London.
3.
Can you help me with this, please?
Yes, I **can.**
4.
Was the play good?
Yes, it **was.** It was excellent.

23

Linda: Is media important for me? Yes, it is. It's really important. My mum's American and so I have lots of American relatives. I get on with them really well but I can't see them all that often so we talk on the computer … a lot. The phone's too expensive so we use the Internet. It's great and it's so cheap. We've all got little videos and we can see who we are talking to. When I've finished talking to them, then I often chat on the Internet, too. I love talking to people who I'd never meet normally.

Jake: Well, I watch TV quite a lot but I'm definitely not a couch potato. I love music and I always watch the music channels when I watch TV. I love to see the videos that go with the songs. Some of them are great. I play in a band and we'd like to make a video, too, some time, so it's great to get ideas from other people.

Elizabeth: I think I use all media a lot. I watch TV, listen to the radio, read newspapers, surf the net but most of all I love books. When I start to read a book, I sometimes can't stop. My parents go crazy and tell me that I need to do sport, too. Usually I use all the other media to find out about books. We don't have a big library in our town and so I really need to find out which books I want them to order for me.

music maniac: Jake; couch potato: –; bookworm: Elizabeth;
super surfer: Linda
Media is important for **Linda** to contact her relatives.
Media is important for **Jake** to get ideas about videos and listen to music.
Media is important for **Elizabeth** to find out more about books.

24

Ann: So did you like it? What did you think?
Mark: I thought it was great. I'm sure you'll get the part. But …
Ann: What? But what?
Mark: Well, I think you should speak a little more slowly. You know, it's more difficult to hear in a theatre, isn't it?
Ann: Yes, that's a good idea. I'll do that.
Mark: And I think it would be better if you moved more.
Ann: What do you mean? I moved all the time.
Mark: Yes, but I mean your arms and your head.
Ann: Hm. I'll think about it.
Mark: And if I were you, I'd stress some of the words more.
Ann: Which words then?
Mark: Well, you said, hm, "I hate you, you … you … idiot you" and I think you should stress the word "hate" more … and maybe "you". You know.
Really show that you hate him. "I hate you, you … you … idiot you."

Ann: So, you'd change everything.
Mark: No, no. Really. You were excellent.

Well, I think you should … → Mark
Yes, that's a good idea. → Ann
What did you think? → Ann
That's rubbish. → *kommt nicht im Dialog vor*
I'll do that. → Ann
I'll think about it. → Ann
And I think it would be better if … → Mark
If you think you're better, why don't you … → *kommt nicht im Dialog vor*
And if I were you, I'd … → Mark

25 Mark thinks that Ann **will** get the part.
He thinks that Ann should speak more **slowly.**
He thinks that Ann should move her **arms/head.**
Ann has to say the words: **"I hate you".**
Mark thinks that Ann **was excellent.**

Unit 6

1 1. plant; 2. coach; 3. seats; 4. tracks; 5. moon; 6. buffaloes

2 1. jo**ur**ney; 2. **r**ailway; 3. noo**d**le; 4. welc**o**me; 5. **seco**n**d** language; 6. del**a**y; 7. prairi**e**
→ Today travelling isn't usually **dangerous.**

3 the world: mankind; foreign countries: traveller; foreign churches: missionary; castle: princess; hospital: paramedic; police station: police officer; people's houses: burglar; fire station: firefighter

4 1. dauern; 2. wegnehmen; 3. mitbringen; 4. mitnehmen/wegnehmen

5 1. She saved me.
2. He's completed the project.
3. He slowed down later.
4. We got bored.
5. I'd recommend this book.

6 1. dangerous; 2. fantastic; 3. disappointing; 4. frightening; 5. annoying; 6. awful

7

A	D	V	I	S	E	P
W	G	K	V	A	R	Z
M	E	N	T	I	O	N
R	S	C	R	E	A	M
E	T	A	S	X	M	H
P	R	O	M	I	S	E
O	E	F	D	O	U	E
R	G	D	W	A	R	N
T	H	P	Y	C	I	Z

1. They **advised** us to find a guide.
2. She **screamed,** "Help, help!"
3. I **warned** him not to swim alone.
4. She later **reported** everything that was said at the meeting.
5. Julie **mentioned** yesterday that you were going to France on holiday.
6. My dad **promised** to give me some money.

8 I worked a lot last summer.
We didn't fight all holiday.
That plant tastes weird.
It didn't rain a lot in Scotland last summer.

9
1. My friend asked, "Would you like to come to France with me?"
2. She always says that France is a fantastic country.
3. "I'd really like to go to France," I told my mum.
4. She said that I could go.

10 Kate phoned last night and she said she **was having** a great time. She said she **loved** it there and that she**'d been** to lots of places. And she said she**'d phone** again tomorrow.

11 The police reported that there had been an accident on the M6.
They said that two lorries had crashed into each other.
They explained that one of the drivers had fallen asleep.
They said they were moving the lorries then.
They added that they hoped the road would be open in two hours.

12 *Kim:* "Hi. I'm sitting in a train. I've just left Madrid. But I didn't sleep there. We can sleep in the train. I'd already spent all my money. I'll be home tomorrow."

1. She said she **was sitting** in a train.
2. She told me that **she'd just left** Madrid.
3. But she said she **hadn't slept** there.
4. She added that they **could sleep** in the train.
5. She said she **had already spent** all her money.
6. She told me **she'd be** home tomorrow.

13 He said he had bought his ticket for that flight the day before.
She said they were flying the next day but they wanted to check in that day.
He said that he often went there because he liked planes.

14 Lucy said she was having a great time there. She said that they had been to Los Angeles the day before and the night before they had watched a play. She said it had been great. She said that her cousin was going there tomorrow and that she was taking her new boyfriend with her. She said she'd tell us/me if he was nice. She added that they were going to the beach the next/following week. She said she hoped she could surf there and that she'd phone us/me again.

15 *Rita:* Hi. Sorry but I can't visit you on Saturday. My grandparents are coming to visit us and they're bringing us a little dog. I'll phone you again. Bye.

→ She said that she couldn't visit us on Saturday. She said her grandparents were going to visit them and they were taking them a little dog.

16 gleich: 1., 3.; später: 2., 4.

17 He says he'll be late because there's been an accident.
He says he can't go on because the road has been closed.
He says that we/I needn't make him any dinner.
He says I'll have to go to judo by bus.

18 She asked me where we/I wanted to go.
She wanted to know how we/I would get there.
She asked if/whether we/I had enough money.
She wanted to know if/whether your parents had agreed.

19 I phoned 999 and I said that **I had seen** an accident. The woman asked me **where I was calling from** and I said that **I was** on the corner of Church Street and London Road. She told me then that the police **were** on their way and asked me **if/whether anybody had been hurt.** I said I **didn't know** but I **thought somebody was trapped** in their car. She said that **they would send** an ambulance and the fire service and asked me **if/whether I was OK** and **what my name was.** It was very exciting.

20 "Where are you going to?"
"Do you like flying?"
"Have you ever been to Australia before?"

21 My mum told me to phone her when I arrive.
My dad advised me to be careful on my bike.
My mum warned me not to get too tired.
My mum told me to look after my bike well.
My dad told me not to ask him for more money.

Lösungen 6

22 He said they **were having** a great time but he asked me t**o send him some more money/if/whether I could send him** some more money. He told me **not to worry about them** and said that **they had arrived** in Cornwall. He said that **he couldn't find** his anorak and asked **if/whether it was** at home.

23 *Policewoman:* There's a fire in the next building.
Please leave the building now.
Don't stop to collect your things.
Are any other people in the building?
Wait here.

She said there was a fire in the next building.
She asked us to leave the building now.
She told us not to stop to collect our things.
She asked if/whether there were any other people in the building.
She told us to wait there.

24 Die beste Zusammenfassung ist c).

25 1. b); 2. a); 3. b); 4. b); 5. c); 6. c)

26 1. line 21; 2. line 40; 3. lines 47/48; 4. line 58; 5. line 60

27 1. I love to swim in the **sea.**
2. He asked me **whether** I like it here.
3. You're coming home tomorrow. **Right?**
4. My front **brake** doesn't work.
5. He's still **weak** because he has been ill.
6. I **rode** a horse yesterday.

28 Emergency 1:
Boy: I've just seen an accident.
Woman: What happened?
Boy: A car hit a boy on a bike.
Woman: Where are you?
Boy: I'm on the corner of Church Road and Park Street.
Woman: Church Road and Park Street. OK. We'll send the police and an ambulance. How many people have been hurt do you think?
Boy: I don't know. Just the boy, I think.
Woman: OK. Don't worry. The police and the ambulance will be there a minute.

1. A car hit a boy.
2. On the corner of Church Road and Park Street.
3. One.
4. The police and an ambulance.

Emergency 2:
Girl: Help! Help! There's a fire. There's a fire.
Woman: OK. I'll send the fire service right away. Where's the fire?
Girl: It's here. In the house next door.
Woman: And where is the house?
Girl: In Market Street.
Woman: What number?
Girl: Er, 12.
Woman: OK. The police, fire services and ambulances will be right there. Has anybody been hurt?
Girl: I don't know.
Woman: Is anybody in the house?
Girl: I don't know.
Woman: Are you in your house?
Girl: Yes.
Woman: Well, go and wait in the street.

1. There's a fire.
2. 12, Market Street.
3. She doesn't know.
4. All services.

29
Girl: Er, hello. Has the 24 gone already?
Boy: No, I don't think so.
Girl: Oh, good. It's probably just late again, isn't it?
Boy: Yeah, it's always late, isn't it?
Girl: You're right there. Last week I waited for half an hour.
Boy: And then two buses came together?
Girl: Exactly. But I hope it isn't too late today. It's so cold.
Boy: Yes, it's only September and it feels like December.
Girl: Oh, Look! There's a bus. Is it the 24?
Boy: No, it's the 15.
Girl: Are you waiting for the 24, too?
Boy: Yes, I'm going into town. And you?
Girl: Yes, I'm going into town, too. I'm going to see 50 Cent.
Boy: Really? Oh, he's great, isn't he?
Girl: Well, I don't know him very well. A friend got the tickets.
Boy: Well, I hope you enjoy it.
Girl: Thanks! Oh, look. Here's our bus.

Boy: Oh no. It isn't stopping.
Girl: Oh. I don't believe it. How annoying!
Boy: Yes, it's terrible, isn't it? Shall we get a taxi together?
Girl: Yes, that's a good idea.

1. a); 2. a); 3. c); 4. c); 5. b)

30

Boy: Yeah, it's always late, **isn't it?**
Girl: **You're right there.** Last week I waited for half an hour.
Boy: And then two buses came together?
Girl: **Exactly.** But I hope it isn't too late today. **It's so cold.**
Boy: **Yes,** it's only September and it feels like December. (…) Yes, I'm going into town. **And you?**
Girl: **Yes,** I'm going to town, too. I'm going to see a band, 50 Cent.
Boy: **Really?** Oh, they're great, **aren't they?**

Revision C (Unit 5–6)

1   **sport:**   athlete, umpire, referee
       royal: princess, empress, knight
       jobs: scientist, paramedic, firefighter

2   1. delay *(die anderen Wörter bezeichnen Geräusche)*
       2. bookworm *(die anderen Dinge kann man essen)*
       3. channel *(bei den anderen handelt es sich um Sendungen)*
       4. traveller *(die anderen Begriffe bezeichnen die Reise selbst)*

3   I want to be an actress but I don't have awesome looks so I don't **get** attention everywhere I go. Next month a famous director is coming to our town and I'm going to **take** the chance to talk to him. He's trying to **raise** money for a charity which he organises. He's going to discuss his ideas on the radio and **give** his opinion on the world's problems. I'm going to be in the studio, too, and I'm going to **get** him to give me a job. I'm going to **make /do** it.

4   I'd always **wanted** to go to New York because some cousins live there. Last summer I **made** it there for the first time. I arrived there at the beginning of July and got a really warm **welcome** from my cousins. They showed me a lot of the city and it is **awesome,** but then they had to go **back** to work so I looked around on my own. They **recommended** some museums and shops to visit and they also **advised** me which parts of town were safe. New York isn't so **dangerous** now but I still **jumped** out of my skin when I heard a noise like a **gun.** It wasn't, of course. Somebody had just opened a bottle of champagne.

5   **I'd already been given** small parts in plays in town when I saw the advertisement for a new TV soap. Actors **were needed** from my town. I **sent** a letter and a photo right away and a few days ago I **was auditioned.** It went well and I still can't believe it, but I'**ve been offered** a part in the soap! It **will be filmed** in our town and it **will be seen** by all my friends and family. I'm very excited. The only problem is that I'm playing a ghost and my face **won't be seen** at all.

> **6**
> 1. Last week a film was made in our town.
> 2. My friends were asked lots of questions by the director.
> 3. I was given a little part in the film.
> 4. We will be shown the film in a few weeks.

> **7**
> The director said that we would be called when it was our turn.
> He asked me/us to act the scene in my/our sides then.
> He asked me/us if/whether I/we had ever acted before.
> He told me/us not to call them and said that they would call me/us.

> **8**
> I said that the train would be at least an hour late and Kate asked if/whether I was going to London, too. I said that I was and that I still had to find somewhere to stay. She told me not to worry and said that I could stay in their house if I liked.

> **9**
> *Daniel:* Hi.
> *Judith:* Hi Daniel. Where are you?
> *Daniel:* I'm at the station.
> *Judith:* Oh. Where are you going?
> *Daniel:* Nowhere. I've just got back from Liverpool.
> *Judith:* Liverpool? Great! Did you meet your cousins?
> *Daniel:* Yeah, I did. And we went on a ferry across the Mersey.
> *Judith:* Nice! So are you going home now?
> *Daniel:* Yes, do you want to come round?
> *Judith:* No, I can't now. But guess what?
> *Daniel:* What? You haven't heard about the casting, have you?
> *Judith:* Yes, I have. The director's assistant called me today.
> *Daniel:* And what did he say?
> *Judith:* He said I've got the part.
> *Daniel:* Oh, wow. Fantastic. Do you want to come to our house to celebrate?
> *Judith:* No, I can't. I've been invited to a party at one of the other actor's houses.
> *Daniel:* Oh. OK.
> *Judith:* But Daniel?
> *Daniel:* Yeah.
> *Judith:* Do you want to come, too?
> *Daniel:* Yeah. Yeah. I'd love to.
>
> 1. Daniel is **at the station.**
> 2. Daniel has been to **Liverpool.**
> 3. Daniel had met **some cousins** there.
> 4. He went on a ferry to **across the Mersey.**
> 5. Judith has heard **about the casting.**
> 6. She's got **the part.**

C Lösungen

7. Daniel invites her **to celebrate at his house.**
8. Judith **can't go.**
9. Judith invites Daniel **to a party.**

10 Judith phoned and I told her I was at the station and that I had been to Liverpool. She asked me if I'd met my cousins there and I said that I had and that I had been on a ferry across the Mersey. I asked if she wanted to come round to my house but she said she couldn't. She then told me that she had got the part in the play. I invited her to celebrate with me at my house but she said that she couldn't. She then asked me if I wanted to go to a party with her and, of course, I said yes.

11
Polizei: Can you tell me what you saw?
Du: **Können Sie uns sagen, was Sie gesehen haben?**
Zeugin: Der Junge auf dem Fahrrad ist die Hauptstraße entlanggefahren, als das Auto einbog.
Du: **The boy on the bike was driving along the road when the car turned into the road.**
Polizei: Did the car driver stop at the stop sign?
Du: **Hat der Autofahrer am Stoppschild gehalten?**
Zeugin: Ja, aber ich glaube, er hat das Fahrrad nicht gesehen. Geht es dem Jungen gut?
Du: **Yes, but she thinks he didn't see the bike. Is the boy OK?**
Polizei: Yes, but the ambulance is still going to take him to hospital now.
Du: **Ja, aber der Krankenwagen bringt ihn trotzdem gleich zum Krankenhaus.**

12 Yesterday afternoon at 12.30 a boy on a bike was hit by a car. The boy was riding down Church Street as the car hit him. A woman who saw the accident said that she thought the car driver hadn't seen the bike. The boy was taken to hospital but it is thought he is fine.

Bildquellennachweis:

- S. 6: Getty Images (MN Chan), München; Picture-Alliance (Rebeca Naden), Frankfurt; Picture-Alliance (epa), Frankfurt
- S. 13: Corbis (Wally McNamee), Düsseldorf; MEV Verlag GmbH, Augsburg; Getty Images (Forster), München
- S. 21: iStockphoto (RF/Vasile Tiplea), Picture-Alliance (Rebeca Naden), Frankfurt; Calgary, Alberta; Getty Images (Powell), München; Marco Polo Agence Photographique (F. Bouillot), Paris.
- S. 23: Getty Images (Forster), München
- S. 27: Avenue Images GmbH (Image Source), Hamburg; Alamy Images RM (AA World Travel), Abingdon, Oxon; AKG, Berlin
- S. 33: Alamy Images RM (IML Image Group), Abingdon, Oxon
- S. 37: AKG, Berlin
- S. 38: Wikimedia Foundation Inc. (PD), St. Petersburg FL
- S. 50: Corbis (Stephane Cardinale), Düsseldorf
- S. 37: AKG, Berlin.
- S. 50: Corbis (Stephane Cardinale), Düsseldorf
- S. 68: Okapia (G. I. Bernard/OSF), Frankfurt; Getty Images (stone/Stephen Johnson), München; Getty Images RF (PhotoDisc), München
- S. 81: Corbis, Düsseldorf
- S. 82: AKG (Rainer Hackenberg), Berlin
- S. 83: Europa-Farbbildarchiv Klammet; Mauritius Images, Mittenwald
- S.110: Avenue Images GmbH (image 100), Hamburg; iStockphoto (RF/Prikhodko), Calgary, Alberta; Fotosearch Stock Photography (Design Pics), Waukesha, WI; Fotosearch Stock Photography (PhotoDisc), Waukesha, WI.

Der Verlag hat sich nach bestem Wissen und Gewissen bemüht, alle Inhaber von Urheberrechten an Texten und Abbildungen zu diesem Werk ausfindig zu machen. Sollte das in irgendeinem Fall nicht korrekt geschehen sein, bitten wir um Entschuldigung und bieten an, gegebenenfalls in einer nachfolgenden Auflage einen korrigierten Quellennachweis zu bringen.

Wissen im Fokus!

Der gesamte Lernstoff der Klassen 5 – 10 in einem Buch:

ISBN 978-3-12-926000-5

Wissen schneller finden: mit Quick-Findern – den extra Inhaltsverzeichnissen für jedes Kapitel.

Wissen besser speichern: mit zusätzlichen Lern-Videos zu besonders schwierigen Themen.

Mit Lern-Videos online!

ISBN 978-3-12-926102-6

ISBN 978-3-12-926042-5

ISBN 978-3-12-926087-6

ISBN 978-3-12-926058-6

ISBN 978-3-12-926101-9

ISBN 978-3-12-926103-3

Im Buchhandel erhältlich. Weitere Informationen unter www.klett.de